Geri Lewis

Marriage is Good
but
Get a Background Check

*A true story about an abused woman's
remarriage to her former husband after thirty-six years;
then, disappointingly, she discovered that he
had been married 12+ times.*

PRESS

Marriage is Good, but Get a Background Check
Barry was married 12 times; I was wife #2 and wife #12.
by Geri Lewis

Printed in the United States of America

ISBN 9781619043589

www.xulonpress.com

Acknowledgements

- I would like to acknowledge my sister, Rose M. Jones who worked with me untiringly to edit my journal entries into a book format. I appreciate you for helping me make this project a success. You allowed the Holy Spirit to guide you with a special anointing each step of the way. Your contribution and support will never be forgotten, and I thank you for your skill and keen eyes on this project.

- The title of my book was given to me by a dear friend, Jacqueline Taylor-Wright, who attended court with me. After court, we went to lunch and as we discussed what transpired in the courtroom, I announced my desire to write a book. As we continued to talk, she said, "Marriage is good, but get a background check". Immediately, I adopted her statement as the title of this book. Jacky you are so appreciated and I will never forget your support.

- My best friend, Brenda DeLotell was with me every step of the way when I was going through the drama with Barry. She encouraged me and supported me in many aspects during my moments of brokenness. She did everything humanly possible to keep me functioning even when I did not feel like it. She allowed the Lord to lead her to keep me grounded. I will never forget your faithfulness to me and your support of my vision is appreciated.

Words cannot express how grateful I am for all of the support that each person contributed to make this project a success. May God Bless you and his face shine richly in your lives. Thank you from the bottom of my heart.

Dedication

This book is affectionately dedicated to my darling deceased mother, Rev. Rosa Lee Cannady, who was my foundation and who truly shaped my life. Her ongoing encouragement for me to get up and fight for what I believed in imparted an inner strength when I fell down in certain areas of my life. I believe that if she were here with me today, she would say, "You fought a good fight, and I applaud your strength and courage to step out on faith."

This book is also dedicated to all of my friends and loved ones who supported me with this project. Many of you had faith in my ability to persevere in spite of tribulation. It was your love that kept me motivated to complete this project.

This book is especially dedicated and designed to help woman like myself who are trapped in a marriage and do not know what is really going on with their mate. It is my hope that men who are experiencing problems in their relationships will be able to glean points from this book as well. It is my prayer that women and men all over the world can benefit from what I am expressing in this book.

Valuable Information for Reading this Non-Fiction Book

- The underlined portions of my journal entries represent my perception of particularly Barry at my initial time of writing. Other underlined portions include fictitious names of my husband's other ten wives who were disclosed during my investigation of the information presented in this book. Their names are listed in the order that he married them.

- The "Awareness" portions, which directly follow the underlined journal entries, are written in bold print throughout this book. These portions give additional opinions and references about the underlined journal entries.

- The "Eye openers" are written in bold and represent my current perception of Barry.

- The names of some of the places and the names of all of the characters in this book are fictitious to protect the innocent.

CONTENTS

Introduction

I recently read an excerpt from a book entitled *How Do I Know If He Is the One to Marry* by Dr. David Gudgel. In this book, there were many references to the two little words "I DO." I can't begin to express to my readers the importance of these two words. These words are filled with awesome implications that people can create a life full of "Love and Happiness", or they can create a life full of "Chaos and Disaster". Saying "I DO" signifies that a man and a woman are entering into a covenant relationship and are promising their love and devotion to one another. It should not be a relationship that is taken lightly or entered into hastily. Both the man and the woman should be convinced that they are spiritually compatible, meaning that their souls are connected and that they are "right and good" for one another. When marrying someone, the operative word is WORK; therefore, each partner should be ready for the challenges of married life.

Before a person says "I DO", it is more important to have had a REAL spiritual connection with the joining of two hearts together with GOD. To go a step further, it is essential to check each other's hearts to see if your companion is willing to say "I DO" to God by being willing to forgive others for their transgressions (Rom. 3:23). It is my hope that you will not allow loneliness or vulnerableness to control your heart or keep you from acquiring a background check on the person who is trying to come into your life. Trust me; it is well worth the effort to do your homework first. There are so many predators out there trying to work their way into successful women and men's lives. When you read this book, you will discover that Barry was a professional in using this scheme. Most of Barry's wives are professional women, such as me, who had significantly hefty retirement funds along with credit cards with huge available lines of credit until Barry drained them dry. Many also had their own homes when they married him. Thank God I did not allow him to coerce me into selling my home although he tried several times. For whatever reason, God would always divert my attention to something else to prevent me from selling my home. I know that he was "looking out" for me in that area.

This is my first book, and I know that it is inspired by God because He actually nudged me to record significant episodes of our marriage into an unused journal lying around the house. I really did not expect our marriage to turn out to be so disastrous. Now, I am aware that it was intended for me to share my experience with others.

I feel that I am a character in a story being written by God. In fact, I am just a nobody who is somebody trying to get the message of abuse out to everybody. I do not have all of the information, but I am listening to Him for instructions. I asked God to turn my pain into HIS POWER, and my gain into Job's wealth so that many abused women and men will become blessed by the contents of this book. He has truly answered my prayer. During my marriage to Barry, I have gained a great deal of strength from numerous challenges, disappointments, confrontations, and tragedies because of God's wisdom, knowledge, and understanding within me during my time of self-expression. I realize that suffering is not always a penalty for sin and that Christians are not exempt from trouble. At this point, my vision will determine my future. I cannot allow myself to be blinded by bitterness. To those who read my book who have had similar experiences, my plea is "not to let your future be held captive by your past". Choices will always have consequences that will determine our destiny. I petition you to be strong in the Lord and the Power of His Might. Take control of your mind and ask God to give you the WISDOM to MOVE FORWARD with your life. As Dr. Robert Schuller always says, "Turn Your Scars into Stars". In other words, "Do Not Get Stuck in the Mud; MOVE FORWARD."

Together Again

(Chapter One)

In the summer of 1967, school was out, the azaleas were in full bloom, and the air was filled with anticipation of an unforgettable summer. Usually, summertime in Richmond Hill, Georgia was a time to gain new friends and explore new adventures, and that summer was no different. Friendships with guys were at the top of the list when we girls talked over the telephone. In one of my many telephone conversations, a female friend, Sherrie, stated that she was interested in dating one of the guys, Barry Lovett. Our entire conversation centered on Barry; her intention was to get his attention as soon as possible. She was extremely fascinated with him to the point that she literally begged and coerced me to contact him for her. I did not feel comfortable with this idea, but because she was my friend, I went along with it.

In the evening later on that week, I contacted him. When he answered the telephone, I identified myself as Germonica Connelly and explained to him that Sherrie asked me to contact him for her. He knew who I was referring to and stated that he was not interested in her. We talked a few minutes more, and he informed me that he had met her at a local nightspot where he was a hired musician in a band and that she had been interested in him since that time. I told him that I would tell her that he was not interested in "talking to her". I made several attempts to discontinue our conversation, but he was adamant about us conversing on the telephone. Barry was a well known musician in the community, and usually women threw themselves on him. My wanting to "hang up" the telephone on him was probably something that Barry was not accustomed to. He played both the keyboard and the trumpet and from what Sherrie told me he was very good at it. He commenced to inform me about his band, where they played, and the success they had had thus far. He was also very proud to note that he was the band leader and was in charge of all of the business aspects for the group. I congratulated him and tried to hang up once again, but he continued to converse with me and stated that he wanted to meet me and would like for me to hear his band play. It felt as though I was fighting hard to get rid of him, but the more I tried to hang up the phone, the more persistent he turned on the charm to get me to hear his band. I relented and allowed him to coerce me into to meeting him.

At school was the first time Barry laid eyes on me. He ranted and raved over how pretty he thought I was and said that if Sherrie looked like me "she could have him". I smiled about the comment and I must admit it made me feel good because I had already had a pretty bad day. He knew just what to say to me. Barry invited me to hear his band play the next Friday night, and, of course, being a young woman at the age of 17, I was not into the "club scene," but I was curious and excited about the idea of going out with who appeared to be a local celebrity. With great anticipation, I was eager to hear his band perform.

Friday night finally came. He came up to the porch of my home and rang the door bell. When I opened the door, I saw a statuesque, tall dark and handsome young man smiling at me. I introduced Barry to my parents, and my infant son, Maurice. After meeting my family, we were off to Club Epsilon.

The club setting was pretty romantic with a large stage that was mounted high in the front of the club where the band sat. He invited me up onto the stage to sit on the stool by him as he played the organ or piano while holding the trumpet in one hand. I was impressed with the band, and I felt honored to be his guest that night. He made me feel so special that night, and I must agree that I felt important because the other young ladies "wanted him." Although part of me felt very bad about going out with him, I did it anyway because he was very persistent, and he made it explicitly clear that he was not interested in my friend. Because I am a considerate and nice kind of a person, I allowed him to manipulate that kind heart of mine. Don't get me wrong; I kept thinking about how I would tell Sherrie about going out with him, but after all of the telephone calls, flowers, fulfilling conversations, and several dates with him at a variety of clubs, and dinner dates, I decided to just tell her the truth about him not "wanting" her and that he pursued me after he convinced me that there was not a chance for the two of them. After much contemplation, I realized that I would not have met Barry if Sherrie had not asked me to contact him to meet her; however, life is full of twists and turns and with fate, I would have probably met him, in any case, as a result of a different situation.

After continually dating Barry for a number of months, our relationship strengthened, and by the end of that same year, Barry asked me to marry him. I agreed to marry him because I was a young mother and wanted a father figure for my son, Maurice, who was a year old at that time. We were married in November of 1968. On the day of my wedding, I had some unsettling in my spirit, but I proceeded with my plans. We had a beautiful church wedding with all accoutrements. The reception was held at my parent's house and was just as stunning.

Not so long after I had married Barry, it was disclosed that **he had already been married to Sondra Chilling, but her parents had the marriage annulled.** He was telling everyone in the community that I was his first wife, but I was, in fact, his second wife. At that time, I wondered why their marriage was annulled because annulments were not a common practice in our community. This should have been a "red flag" to check out the reason for their failed marriage, but I was young, in love, and enjoying the first few days of our marriage.

Our first residence was called Felton Gardens. We were happy and content living there for a couple of months, but one day, when he came home from work, he said to me out of the blue, "We are moving in a small house that my grandparents own behind their house." That same day he started packing things without any previous notice to me. I knew he was crazy when he did that to me. Everything changed when we married. Almost immediately after we married I became pregnant and he stopped taking me out. I felt as if I were in a nightmare that I did not care to be in. Barry became very mean and hateful towards me, and he wanted to control me. I thought this was my punishment for not being a faithful friend to Sherrie. I started digging deep down into my soul for answers as to how I got into this situation. I asked God to forgive me for my actions. I felt as though I had a grasp on my actions, but at this point, Barry's actions were questionable. In addition to playing in the band, Barry worked a day job. He played his weekend gigs at the club and probably wanted me to live in the house behind his grandparents so that they could keep an eye on me to make sure that I did not go anywhere. He stayed out late almost every night and left me at home "to look at four walls" after I said "I DO". It had gotten to the point that either he began to stay out extremely late or stayed out to the next morning. When he came home, he argued with me for no reason at all. Barry was drinking and partying quite often, and his problem became so awfully serious that my mother decided that she would take me home with her to keep him from fighting me.

At my parent's house, I felt more secure. My son, Maurice, was already living with my parents because my mother had indicated that Barry had been very mean to him and that she was not fond of my husband because of his bad attitude. At that time, to make matters worse, I was pregnant and miserable; Barry had deceived me so badly that I wanted to kill him. Being young and somewhat immature, I did not ask a great deal of questions. I was in love and I did not realize that I could not live on love alone. Barry was a great actor. He deceived me to believe that he would be a good provider and an excellent husband. Before we were married, he would constantly tell me, "I love you with all of my heart". These were ALL LIES from the pit of hell. Even though I had had my son, Maurice, when

17

I met Barry, I was not a partying young woman in and out of clubs all the time. I was a good looking mysterious woman who was exciting and challenging to him. I was a fresh face that other young men were attracted to me as well. For these reasons, I feel that he was attracted to me in the first place. After he conquered my heart and impregnated me with our child, he seemed to be no longer interested in me.

On March 29, 1969 our son, Tyrese, was born. He was five months old when his dad and I were divorced in September of 1969. I applied for child support through the Department of the Child Support Enforcement Division (DCSED) and was granted $11.50 a week. To my surprise, Barry was not in favor of paying that small amount of money to support his own child. As a matter of fact, he played his little acting game and came to court on crutches looking for sympathy from the judge in an effort to escape paying child support. This act was lowdown and dirty, but his true character surfaced when he did this. Within my heart, I knew that I could not trust him and did not need him in my life. I made up my mind to be both the father and the mother in Tyrese's life because his father was not trustworthy. I loved our son with all of my heart and tried to give him the best life possible. I was an industrious mother who sent both of my children to private school. I was not about to sink into misery because of this failed marriage. With faith in God to help me along with my parent's encouragement, I was able to focus upon beginning a new life for me and my children.

It was in 1977, several years later, before I saw Barry again. As a matter of fact, I had married Frederick McCormick that year, and we later moved to Denver, Colorado. Unfortunately, my marriage to Frederick was not a good one either. He was mean and violent as well, and our marriage only lasted 7 years. I could not believe that I "blew it" once again in choosing the wrong man.

I needed to recuperate from this nasty ordeal. For this reason, my children and I left Denver and moved back to Richmond Hill. I was 36 years old and my children were between the ages of 15 and 19 years of age. I was desperate to regain a stabilized lifestyle for my children and provide the necessary things for them; therefore, I decided to enter college to work on a degree. My thoughts were solely on making life better for my children, but my children's minds reverted to establishing relationships with their fathers. Within months after returning home, Tyrese decided to look for his father who was now 37 years old. Finally, he found him and discovered that he had been married five times. At that time, his dad's marriages did not seem to bother him. After all, Barry is still his dad. Tyrese visited his dad a few times and noticed that he had some issues. He, especially, observed that his dad did not stay married to any of his wives.

In retrospect, I can recall that **Barry's first wife, Sondra,** did not have any children from him, but at the age of 18, **I became Barry's second wife and the mother of his first child**; the **third wife, Betty, birthed**

18

a daughter; the **fourth wife, Holly, birthed two daughters from him**; his marriage to **Vera, his fifth wife,** was brief and just as most of the wives, **she did not have any children from him**. Barry was a rolling stone and lived in the fast lane. In 1987, he did not waste any time before he invited Danielle to live with him; they had a son together, but they never married. Back then, this **living arrangement with Danielle was considered a "common law marriage",** and it was honored because they lived together for two and a half years; therefore, **she was considered his seventh wife**. Because **she had "little Barry"**, she took him to court for alimony and child support. She won the case and had him restrained from the property for at least a year due to several acts of abuse towards her. It is very out of the ordinary that *Barry had all of the wives live in the same house except for the first four.* I spoke with a woman the other day that attended my church, and she informed me that her aunt and uncle lived on the same street as Barry. They called him the "crazy man because he keeps changing wives". I wish I had spoken to her before I married him the second time around. Barry told me that he married, **Patty, wife number eight,** who was a very young girl because he needed her assistance in taking care of his grandparents who lived with him for a short while when they were ill. He was indeed an opportunist. He had a hidden agenda in his multiple marriages to these women, and his most frequent motive was "for money". I had the pleasure of speaking with **wife number nine, Ginger**, when I was going through my second divorce from Barry. She called me long distance and stated that he was the worst kind of husband and that he was very mean and manipulative. She also said that he does not need another woman he needs a man. I informed her about his manipulation and the abuse he perpetrated upon me, and she said that when she saw me with him at church, she was wondering how long it would last. Ginger also said that his wives usually go to Tennessee and Niagara Falls with him. Barry told me that I was the only woman that he had ever taken there except for the wife before me. He is a GREAT LIAR and ACTOR and I cannot believe I allowed him to deceive me like he did once again. **Wife number ten, Stella,** was my greatest asset during my court proceedings. Stella wrote an affidavit and said that he promised to take care of her and her son, but he abused them mentally and emotionally as well. During their marriage, he locked the refrigerator and changed the locks on the door so that she could not get into the house. She affirmed that Barry did not want her son around because he disliked him. He even tried to send her son to New York to be with his father. Stella avowed that before she came into his life, she had had a comfortable lifestyle, but when he rejected her and requested that she get out of his life, she was almost facing bankruptcy. As you can see, Barry's MO is to convince his wives to go on trips with him, but they end up spending their money for almost everything. He might pay for a couple of small things, but that's all. With **wife number eleven,**

Betty, yes, he married two women whose name is Betty, but this one was seven years older than Barry. He divorced her in December of 2005. Wife number eleven Betty, was not a happy camper either when he decided to divorce her. He lied to me about what she had done to him, and I bought into his lies. First of all, I did not realize that he was married to her when he started courting me in June of 2005. He told me that their relationship had been "over" for a long time, but they just hadn't gotten their divorce yet. As time passed, and our relationship became stronger, Barry became more seriously involved with me and expressed a desire to be in my life for a long time. That's when he asked me to marry him. Little did I know that **even though I had been wife number two that I would also become wife number twelve.**

In viewing his marriages, I realized that he had established an MO, mode of operation, whereas his tract record to remain in a marriage was about two and one-half to three years. It is possible that once or twice he may have remained a little longer in a marriage but only because of ULTERIOR MOTIVES. Another point is that age was not a factor in these marriages. Wife number six, Patty, was ten years younger than he, and Betty was seven years older than he. He married three women who were considerably older and three women who were considerably younger. The other wives were within two to three years his age. A final point is that Barry admits that he has an estranged daughter who he named after his sister, but he later decided not to claim this daughter for whatever reason. It is my understanding that she looks like one of his other daughters.

The second time Barry began to pursue me, I was blindfolded about the facts involving these other marriages, and as a result, I was conned into becoming a good friend to him once again. The renewal of our relationship was set into motion when our grand daughter, Brigitte a fifth grader, graduated from elementary school. She invited both of us to attend her graduation, but we were unaware of the other's invitation. When the ceremony had ended, he asked if he could take us to lunch and we agreed. Brigitte, her parents, Barry and I went to Ruby Tuesday's for lunch to celebrate Brigitte's graduation. As we were about to part, he asked if he could contact me, but I insisted on knowing his reason. He convincingly stated that he just wanted to talk to me about a few things. I assumed that those "few things" would include keeping in touch because of his son and granddaughter; therefore, I said "Okay". Later, that same day, he contacted me. His whining conversation centered on how poorly everyone was treating him and how badly his family members used him. As if this wasn't enough, he continued to gripe about how distraught he was about his job that he had worked for many years. It was as if he had no direction, but because he was very sweet and charming towards me, I felt compelled to talk to him about the Lord and how God gives us peace. Soon after this conversation, we had Bible Study and prayed together at my home on a regular basis. He also came over to my house very early every morning. We would walk around the lake and talk about God's grace. Then, he began to pray out loud for both of us. I gave him books to read along with scriptures from the Bible so that we could discuss them later. I will never forget telling him about Jeremiah 29:11 which states: "I know the plans that I have towards you "thoughts of peace and not of evil" to give you a hope and a future or expected end." He said that he understood what I was trying to tell him and that he was hoping to get his joy back. For several months, we had had some very interesting conversations over a variety of topics, especially, topics from the Bible. Then, he finally asked me out on a date. I felt reluctant about this, but he was Tyrese's father, and I felt obligated to bring him into a more peaceable state of mind. To add to all of this, he was complaining about back problems, and because I had a Jacuzzi on my deck, I allowed him to get into it from time to time. We became good friends.

In July of 2005, I informed him that I was going to attend my family's reunion in Myrtle Beach, and he asked if he could attend it with me. He immediately disclosed that his money was low and that, in fact, he did not have any funds at all. At that time, I did not recognize his python spirit, a person that sucks everything out of you. I truly felt that he had had an unfortunate season, and because of my good nature, I tried to help him through it. For this reason, I went to my bank and withdrew some funds and gave him some large bills so that he could enjoy some time away from his mother and his sister who, according him, had radically mistreated him to the point that he did not like them. From my conversations with Barry, I discovered that he did not have a loving and caring relationship with his mom who had been placed in a nursing home with dementia. Tyrese and I thought that was a bit much for Barry not to visit his ailing mother, but he was so adamant about it that we just went along with the craziness and stayed away from his mother and sister while we were together.

After dating Barry for a year, I assumed that he had improved immensely so I told him that I was so proud of him for trusting God and letting go of his worries. He appeared to have gained great peace. During the course of our dating this time around, he stopped attending the church where he had been a member and church musician and began attending a non-denominational church where I had become a member. He asserted that attending the new church gave him new life; the people were friendly and warm, and the pastor seemed personable. Because of his positive experience, we continued to attend church together on a regular basis. Barry's seemingly commitment to God won my heart. I had longed for a true man of God, and he assured me that he was "sold out to God" by his actions, dedication, and faithful service to God. Barry knew that I wanted a man who loved God, and he played his role very well. I truly believed that he was real in loving God's WORD as he did. I grew to love him once again; he began to send me flowers and romanced me to the fullest extent. Most of all, he seemed to express a deep love for God.

After one year of dating, he asked me to marry him a second time around, and on June 2, 2006, we were married again. We were married on a Friday morning at the church in the presence of our son, Tyrese, his wife Cherlyn, and their daughter, Brigitte. Before we were married, Tyrese told me that I should not marry his dad because he had had multiple marriages. He also tried to convince me that his dad and I were totally different people. I heard Tyrese's words of warning about his father, but I told him that his dad had made some major changes in his life and that I believe he would be a good husband to me this time around. Both of my sons, Maurice and Tyrese, were against this marriage, but I followed my heart and married him anyway. There was, however, something in my spirit that lead me to journal my relationship with Barry. For this reason, I commenced my journaling on June 4, 2006. It is as follows.

Enduring in spite of the Storm

(Chapter Two)

June 4, 2006 on Sunday evening @ 6:42pm—**Dear Journal**, I never thought I would write in this journal, but today, the Holy Spirit nudged me to do so, and here I am writing in my journal book that I have had for over seven years. I guess marrying Barry a second time has had a great deal to do with keeping track of our lives together. We were married two days ago at the ages of 57 and 58. Wow! It was four decades ago when we were first married at the ages of 17 and 18 years old. Over the years, my life's experiences compelled me to have a relationship with God and to fellowship with others. I made a promise to be in church as often as possible; therefore, this morning we went to church together for the first time as a married couple. At the marriage ceremony this past Friday, our pastor reminded us that marriage is a sacred institution and a covenant joining a man and a woman as "one" by their consent to pledge their faith to one another through giving and receiving rings. At church this morning, the pastor announced our marriage to the congregation. Then, he requested that all married couples come up front for prayer. He was so happy about the fact that Barry and I rediscovered one another after many years of divorce. He told the congregation that God was awesome to bring us back together after that many years. When we went to his office prior to getting married, during our conversation, he discovered that Barry played the organ. As a result, he announced to the congregation that God was going to use Barry mightily. I am so proud of my husband because now, he may become a musician for the church.

June 11, 2006 on Sunday @ 11:50pm—Dear Journal, I have been married to Barry since June 2nd, and I am very happy at this very moment. We started our day with prayer and a light breakfast. Then, we went to church this morning. <u>Today, the pastor had all of the new members to come up</u>

and Barry was in the number. I am feeling so proud of him. **He has come a long way since last summer (Eye opener: He was probably acting).**

June 12, 2006 on Monday morning @ 11:00am—Dear Journal, We began our day with a delightful fellowship breakfast under the car porch. The menu was boiled eggs and cereal bars with coffee. We kissed and spoke of how happy we are. God is really doing a work in our lives. Last night was very special; we connected a little closer to each other. I was beginning to wonder why he did not pursue me as often as I thought he would; so, I am pleased with last night. He even told me that he never experienced this kind of closeness to anyone and that he loved me with all of his heart. We talked about "trust" being the number one factor in a relationship; we both stated that we trusted each other and wanted our lives to be one of trust **(Eye opener-Our relationship was full of distrust, insincerity, deceit, manipulation etc.—just plain spousal abuse).**

June 26, 2006—Dear Journal, Barry and I were invited as guests to attend his daughter Heather's engagement party. This would be our first trip as a married couple. We traveled to Atlanta with Tyrese, Cherlyn and Brigitte, and lodged at the Hilton in College Park, Georgia for four days and three nights. While we were there, we went to a Braves' game; the first night they lost 3-2. We also had the pleasure of dining at the Sundial Restaurant on Friday night. After dinner, Tyrese treated us to a carriage ride. Barry told me that his money was low before we left for Atlanta; I accommodated him with the necessary funds for the hotel. I also paid for our expensive dinner at the restaurant **(Awareness - Red flag-probably "user issues").** The third night was the engagement party. Everything was very nice, and we had a lot of fun. Barry and Tyrese furnished the music and speakers and Tyrese was the DJ of the evening. Barry stated that he was in pain and said that the carriage ride probably initiated the pain. It is really interesting that Barry is on disability for back pain, but he is always working in the yard and cooking meals. **(Awareness - Red flag - probably "deceit issues").** He said that he needed to keep busy in order for him not to dwell on the pain. I pray for Barry a great deal and I believe God for his healing and that my husband would begin to speak positive words over his life. I have received my healing by speaking positive words over my sickness, and today I am healed. I pray for him to walk into that truth also.

July 19, 2006 – Dear Journal, I am very sad today because we were not intimate at all. It has been several days without intimacy because of Barry's back pain. I love him very much, and I need to express that love. My prayer is "GOD please touch him with your power and cause him to want his healing." I believe he thinks that if he asks you for his healing, his disability checks will discontinue, **(Awareness - Red flag- probably "insincerity issues").** I know that you are not a God who that will cause him to regress. I know that you will protect him from all hurt, harm, and danger. I want unity to become the focus of our relationship so I am praying for all areas of our life to be blessed, particularly, our family. His daughters' Heather and Evon treat me decently; therefore, I am looking forward to spending time with them soon.

July 20, 2006—Dear Journal, I have been trying to keep a picture perfect house along with keeping our clothes, linen, and towels clean. If I could name one thing that I am grateful for today, it would be that I am grateful for my husband's cooking skills. He prides himself as a chef and often cooks mouth-watering meals for me daily. The one thing that I regret is that I have gained weight, and we are not intimate enough for newlyweds. We have begun walking around the park once again and that is a good thing because we both need exercise. **(Flashback to July 4th)** — My sister and her husband from Florida came to visit us for the fourth of July and stayed from Monday through Wednesday. During their stay, Barry's menu the first day was rotisserie' chicken, a roast, and crab casserole. The next day, the menu included Crowder peas and fried red snapper. They said the food was finger licking good. Upon leaving, they acknowledged that we were great hosts and that they enjoyed themselves immensely **(Flashback ends).** — Next week, we are visiting Florida. I have been invited to sing on program at my sister's church. I have already made reservations at the Hilton Garden Inn because Barry did not want to stay in their house because other family members would be there also. I paid for us to stay in the hotel in Highland **(Awareness - Red flag- probably "user issues").** I thought it would be good to stay with them because they have a four bedroom home and their children are grown and have their own homes, but Barry is quite private. Since his birthday is this month, the hotel may be a good way to celebrate his special day.

July 26, 2006— Dear Journal, Barry and I were in Florida from July 22nd to the 25th. Everything went well in Florida except we were not intimate. I am beginning to wonder if his physical challenge is somewhat psychological because no matter how much a man hurts he desires his wife some times **(Awareness - Red flag- At that time, I detected that he seemed to have this issue).** I guess I need to pray for restoration in this area. God is indeed a healer because he healed me. On our way back from Florida, we had an argument. The results of the argument caused him to be angry with me while driving back home. As a matter of fact, he remained angry with me for a few days because I asked him why we are never intimate. I do not understand why this would cause him to get angry **(Awareness - Red flag probably "psychological issues").**

August 1, 2006—Dear Journal, Last evening was quite different from the usual. Barry and I had dinner (left-overs from Sunday) when I returned from the salon. We discussed our relationship problems over dinner tonight, and I told him that we needed to become a "tight fist" to disallow negative intervention to enter into our lives. He said that he understood and proceeded to compliment me on my youthful look. He also said that he is completely satisfied with me. We watched a little television; then, we retired for bed. Before going to sleep, I read a portion of a chapter called "Walking in the Light" from the book entitled *Prayers that Prevail*. Then, I prayed, and I asked him to pray. I prayed for oneness and for us to walk into our divine destiny. After that Barry popped the question, "If you could be anywhere right now, where would you want to be?" At 11:00 at night, I replied, "I would want to be right where I am which is home." I reversed the question back to him and he said, "at home**.**" Then, I told him that I missed being with family and friends and that I prayed for them on a regular basis. He became very upset even enraged with me for making this comment, and responded, "You should have married them; you lied to me. I built the deck and put a Jacuzzi outside for your comfort and you are telling me that you miss other people." I really did not understand what he was talking about. Missing family and friends did not have anything to do with my marriage to Barry**.** I have tried over and over again to analyze his behavior but could not make any sense out of it **(Awareness - Red flag-probably "psychological issues").** He is not talking to me today, and I am just keeping quiet and asking God to handle this crazy situation. We have been married for two months and now I am reminded of the PEACE that I had when I was single. I told Barry that one of the most important things in my life was to have PEACE and he promised that he would not disturb that peace. Now I am wondering if I made another mistake in marrying Barry second time **(Awareness - Red flag-probably "psychological issues").**

August 2, 2006 –Dear Journal, Today is a good day. I woke up this morning feeling nothing but "total peace" in my soul. I thank God for all of the joy he is giving me in spite of my obstacles. I am grateful that my husband asked me to breakfast on Thursday morning and whatever that was that came over him the other day is done with for good. I bought him a wedding song book with Ave' MARIA in it at the book store the other day as a piece offering to mend us back together again. I knew that he always wanted that piece of music so that he could learn that song for future engagements. My girlfriend and I were at the Mall, and we walked and talked about Barry today**.** I told her that we had only been married for two months and we were having some problems **(Awareness - Red flag- "marital issues").** I was too embarrassed to share too much information with her.

August 3, 2006—Dear Journal, The next morning, Barry and I spent the morning together. <u>I treated him to breakfast at Cracker Barrel. Later that night, Barry and I attended my girlfriend's birthday party at Outback restaurant downtown. I told him to order whatever he wanted and that it was my treat; so, he ordered lamb and said it was scrumptious</u> **(Awareness - Red flag-probably "user issues").** The fellowship was enjoyable and while we were there, Barry apologized to me about his behavior the other day, and I accepted. We are getting along very well once again. <u>He asked me to plan a trip for my birthday and said that he wanted me to visit Cherokee, NC and go see the play *Unto These Hills*; he also wanted to go to Pigeon Forge, Tennessee, and travel to Atlanta to attend the Braves game</u> **(Awareness - Red flag- probably "user issues").**

August 11, 2006 @ 12:00pm — Dear Journal, Barry and I have already had the most wonderful time vacationing in North Carolina and Tennessee. Now, we are in Atlanta, Georgia on a Friday night. We are lodging in the Hilton Hotel in College Park. Barry is sound asleep as I journal our activities. We left home on the 9th of August and have stayed at some of the best hotels in town and I am not so happy. <u>I have tried to set aside my feelings, but it is so hard to ignore that we are not intimate with one another</u> **(Awareness - Red flag-probably "psychological issues").** I told Barry over and over again that if we never connect we will not get closer to one another. <u>Information goes into one of his ears and right out of the other</u> **(Awareness - Red flag-seemingly "stubborn issues").** He enjoys taking these trips but we really never enjoy the full pleasure as married couples should.

May 1, 2007 – Dear Journal, It has been about eight months since I have made any entries into my journal. <u>I guess it is because the marital road has been very very bumpy for several months now and I have attempted to just throw in the towel on a few occasions I have been so discouraged and downright desponded about certain areas of my marriage</u> **(Awareness - Red flag- "marital issues").** We are beginning to bond much closer together once again. Our winter was fairly good with one major argument. His outbreaks are always over something very silly. <u>For example, we would argue over whether I closed the door correctly or whether I put his shampoo back into his shower stall. He is a very immature person and gets angry at the drop of a dime. I never know when the "wolf" is going to come out of him. It is quite frightening to live with someone like this</u> **(Awareness - "Red flag-probably "psychological issues").**

Total Deception
(Pretending and Acting, His Greatest Gifts)
(Chapter 3)

May 12, 2007— **Dear Journal,** last night at the Italian Club, I attended a rehearsal dinner given by my girlfriend, Betsy, for her son and his bride-to-be. Barry and our granddaughter, Brigitte, were also guests at this event. We were really enjoying ourselves, but after a short while Brigitte had become very ill, and it became necessary for us to leave. The next day, we attended the wedding at St. Andrew's Catholic Church. While we were there, Barry told me that he did not feel well, but he would try "to hang in there with me". I will continue to pray for his healing. I believe with all of my heart that if he gets off those oxycontin pills, he will automatically feel better. Those pills are doing more harm than good to him. I believe that once a person consumes so many pills, their immune system shuts down having so much of it in their system. **(Eye opener: Barry's problem was not only the pills it was deeper—it was probably "psychological").** In addition to this, Barry carries a great deal of unforgiveness in his heart. He is constantly talking about how badly his mother treated him as a child and that he will never have a relationship with her because of some of the things that she had said to him. I used to talk to him about forgiving her, but he did not want to hear it. He would always tell me that he has forgiven her, but he did not want to see her. He even went so far as to say that if she died, he will not attend her funeral. **(Eye opener: A man's first love is his mother; if a man can not love his own mother, he can not love a woman. Barry seemed to possess "psychological issues").** I cannot understand this kind of behavior because my family has issues all the time, but we know how to forgive and move on with our lives. We realize that at the end of the day we are still a family, and that it is essential that we find a way to continue loving one another. To add to all this drama, Barry has revealed that he hates his sister Marsha with a passion. He is always talking about what she did to him as well. As a matter of fact, I found out that he does not like too many people. I am continuing to search for ways to bring him into the righteous ways of God. I demonstrate love and affection towards him but he rejects me on a regular basis. Most of the time, he would rather fight than love. I believe his pain involves more than just his back pain. **(Awareness: I perceived that Barry was hurting inside from relationship issues with his mother and sister. He was probably suffering from the "psychological" issues of unforgiveness and malice).**

May 15, 2007 – Dear Journal, Barry wanted to go on a cruise back in April of this year and to be specific it was the *Glory Carnival* that he went on with his last wife Betty. He said that he did not enjoy it at all with her and wanted to share that experience with me. Barry asked me to book this cruise and as always being the submissive wife that I am, I booked it but ended up paying for it as well. He has a way of getting me to do things and promise to pay me back and never does **(Awareness - Red flag: probably "user issues").** I was expecting him to give me my money back by now; I guess I can forget that. **(Awareness: Barry never intended to reimburse those funds to me).** I think there are a series of things going on with him, but I am going to try to make our relationship work. **(Awareness - Red flag: Even then, I knew that he had some issues.)** We met a woman on the cruise by the name of Marie who sat right next to Barry every night on our seven day cruise. I do not feel that it was just a coincidence that she sat by him because she had some back problems and shared with him that she had been taking pain shots for the last five years. She stated that the shots had helped her tremendously. She also stated that it worked; I wanted him to try doing the same thing, but he is afraid of pain. I told him that short term pain is better than long term pain, but he could not digest that information. God meant for his ears to hear that testimony. About one and a half weeks ago, Barry experienced some chest pain so I insisted that he see a doctor. He went to the emergency room. They scheduled a nuclear stress test for him to do. I hope that they examine him for more than just a stress test. Actually, I am hoping they find this controlled substance in his system and take him off of the oxycontin pills. **(Awareness: At that time, I was very naïve to assume that it was only his meds that caused him to be an abuser.)**

May 23, 2007 — Dear Journal, Today is Wednesday and I am continuing to pray for completeness so that the fruits of the spirit will reside in my marriage. I sometimes wonder if he understands that I need to connect spiritually and physically. As I have told him over and over again nothing in the world can replace the intimacy that married couples should have together. One thing that puzzles me is that Barry constantly complains about back pain; yet, he cuts our grass and two of our neighbors grass all in one day and then he would sometimes come in the house and cook dinner shortly afterward. I wondered why he did not complain about back pain at that time? I would often times contact my daughter-in-law and explain that situation to her. She would say thank God you know how to handle that because you had been alone for a long time. Sometimes, I think it is ED (erectile dysfunction), but he would not tell me due to embarrassment; therefore, he continues to tell me it is back pain **(Awareness - Red flag- seemingly "deceit")**. "Lord, what can I say or do to get this problem solved once and for all? I am not the kind of woman that would cheat on him, but after being sexless for about ten years, I am a woman with great needs in that area. Everything else is better at least for right now. I love him and he loves me, but sometimes, I feel that he is afraid to express his love for some reason, "(**Awareness - Red flag- probably "psychological issues"**). On another note, our children are doing fine. Tyrese is our heart; he is special because out of all of the children, he loves us with action, and he is reliable. He has taught his dad a number of technological skills on the computer. This makes Barry feel good about the knowledge he has gained from Tyrese. Now, Barry is able to scan, download music, crop pictures, attach documents, and maneuver many other functions on a computer. He brags about his knowledge to everyone. **(Awareness - Red flag- probably "esteem issues")**. He is extremely proud of Tyrese and all of his accomplishments of being a responsible family man and employee. We thank God that Tyrese and Cherlyn are working together rather than against each other. Brigitte is going to summer camp this summer at the Habersham Street Y.M.C.A., and we are praying for her to develop into a very mature and responsible teen-ager. By the way, the stress test came back negative and we are happy about that today**. (Flashback to last Saturday)-** Barry and I performed at the Widows Conference on last Saturday and everyone appeared to have enjoyed my songs which were "Say the Name" and "We Shall Behold Him" of which I sang with an accompaniment tract; Barry accompanied me on the last song which was "Heavenly Fathers' Children".

June 19, 2007—Dear Journal, I am sitting here thanking God Almighty for all of His many blessings. In spite of some opposition, since my last visit to journaling, **(Flashback to June 4)** we traveled to Atlanta June 4th to attend a Braves game and a Broadway play entitled "*Dream Girls*". June 2nd was our first anniversary, but because Barry had to play in the church band Sunday, we left on Monday, June 4th. Our first year as a married couple was very rough, but I have faith that we will make it through our storms. We arrived in Atlanta and stayed at the Omni Hotel downtown. We were not very pleased with the room, but we lodged there anyway because of our schedule. The hotel stated that they will make it up to us later. Overall, the trip was fantastic. In the meantime, I am still spending a great deal of money towards our trips; I paid for the gas, lodging, tickets for these events, and most of the eating expenses **(Awareness -I realized that Barry is definitely a "user")**. On the brighter side, Barry has made quite a change in the past few months. We can actually talk and have a conversation without having an argument. I feel that God is really making the crooked places straight and the rough places smooth. **(Eye opener: Barry only seems to have changed; he is an accomplished actor).** However, I still believe God for miraculous healing in his body. We go on trips and I spend big money when we go and we also stay at the best hotels, but our sex life is horrible. **(Awareness: Barry is probably a "user and an abuser").** Father's Day was good for him; he enjoyed the children very much; Tyrese gave him another Braves hat and two shirts. He felt blessed by Tyrese's gracious actions of love. His daughter, Evon, called to wish him a happy father's day. It seems as though God has taken control of his feelings of hurt as far as his girls are concerned. He was talking about them very badly for a long time because he always feels as though they are controlled by their mother and he hates that. I think that my prayers are working so I will continue to ask God to bless every area of our lives.

June 28, 2007 @ 5:20 pm – Dear Journal, Today is a good day for us, and yesterday was also a good day except we had a disagreement last night over something trivial. It was crazy to me (very small) so I ignored him. He called me on his way home from Bible study and told me that he refused to let our marriage go to hell as he did with his other marriages. I really appreciated that he made that comment to me; it meant so much to me to hear him say that. Today, about 12:00 we had had an awesome prayer time together; we prayed over our children's pictures i.e. Maurice, Tyrese, Cherlyn, Brigitte and Nique. He did not want to pray over his girls pictures today. He is not completely free from the issue with them being controlled by their mother. **(Awareness- Red Flag – probably "unforgiveness issues"; he was blocking his blessings).** He is better but not completely free yet; so, I am going along with him for peace sake. We prayed over our wallets and for our barns to always to be full. **(Awareness: At the rate of spending money at Barry's request, Barry's barn (pocket) was the only one that had a chance to be filled because my barn was continually being depleted.)** I also prayed that "Barry would be healed from the crown of his head to the soles of his feet and that God Almighty would speak to his heart and mind. God, you promised us that if we delight ourselves in you, you will give us the desires of our heart. Thank you for the VICTORY!!! AMEN."

August 9, 2007 — Dear Journal, It has been a while since I have written. **(Flashback to events in July 2007)** — We left home on the 19th of July to visit Atlanta and spent two nights in a presidential suite that the Omni blessed us with because they made a mistake June. This was a dream room with all the special amenities in it— the garden tub, the executive dining table, the king sized bed with everything that you can imagine in it, and the beautiful scenery from the top floor. After we left Atlanta, we lodged in Pittsburg for one night, and then to Niagara Falls where we were guests at the Marriott Hotel. It was a wonderful experience for both Barry and I; it was so beautiful.

After spending two nights in Niagara Falls, we decided to visit Washington DC where we were guests in the Hilton Hotel. This was a breathing taking experience! On our first day in Washington, we wanted to see the White House, and to our surprise, we were blessed to see President Bush and First Lady Laura Bush welcome eleven countries. We also had the distinct honor of viewing Ambassadors and Heads of State entering into the WHITE HOUSE. Barry and I connected in a very special way on July 1st, 4th, and 20th of 2007; Praise the Lord what a great change. His health problems are improving. **(Eye Opener: It is possible that his guilt of being a "user" overtook him to the point that he wanted to demonstrate a "caring demeanor" towards me. It is my belief that our connection was not so genuine; it was all about "using and control").** I will need many more episodes such as this; this is the most activity we have had this year. I know my prayers are prevailing and this is living proof.

August 9, 2007 – Dear Journal, I will be 59 years old tomorrow. I decided to walk alone at the mall today just to do a little thinking about my life as a married woman. I am remembering how Barry courted me when we met at Brigitte's graduation in 2005. He was so kind and sweet to me. I saw him as a totally different person from when we were together as teen-agers. I never thought in my wildest dreams that I would be married to him at this time in my life. Although he came into my life with a spirit of not having the "Peace of God" within him, he treated me with kindness and respect. At that time, I was enduring a very vulnerable stage in my life because I went through a situation on my job that involved a great deal of disappointment for me, and as a result, I went into a state of depression. My depression caused me to become disabled. Subsequently, when Barry and I met, I was open to his sweet kind spirit towards me. He was not in the best frame of mind about God and the Peace that He gives us, but he seemed happy about being with me. Today is a day of reflection for me because my birthday will be tomorrow. He promised to take care of me if I married him, but he is not doing a great job with that promise. He also stated that he Loved God, but he became a lot slacker after we were married. **(Awareness - Beware of "con artists" who say or do anything to get you interested, but after he captures your heart, he puts you through countless changes that make your life a living hell.)** He seems to want me to spend my money for everything and always announce that he is broke or low on funds. I always come through for him because I want to make him happy. **(Awareness - When you know that you are being used, do not succumb by pleasing your partner just to get along with him. You're making him become more controlling. You're in a power struggle.)**

December 30, 2007 @ 7:30am — Dear Journal, It has been four months since I have expressed my thoughts. Today is Brigitte's 14th birthday. WOW! She is getting older, and I am feeling older because she is growing up. I felt so compelled to write today because so many things have occurred since my last journal entry. Barry has become very irritated with the band at the church and feels as if the pianist is very demanding. He is also disturbed with the manner in which the choir leader is handling the choir selections as well. He continues to complain about his pain in his body, but I decided not to pray with him or anything else because he has been complaining that I talk about the Word too much. The only thing I can do is pray for him. **(Flashback to September 2007)** His sister stopped by one September evening to tell Barry that his mother was about to part with her house. I was proud that he handled this business without arguing with her; however, he told her that she was not allowed to visit our house any-more. The next time she came to the house, he called the police on her. He really dislikes this particular sister. **(Awareness - Barry continued to hold grudges and harbor unforgiveness against his relatives; he con-tinued to block his blessings**). According to 1st Corinthians, Chapter 13, verse 13, "and now abide faith, hope, love, these three; but the greatest of these is love."

December 31, 2007—Dear Journal, Barry and I rode on River Street tonight, but today, we went walking at the mall to keep our health issues in order. We both are type II diabetics, but we are doing well with control-ling it with exercise and eating a proper diet. Both of us have lost weight. **(Flashback to October)** In October, we went to the Coastal Empire Fair and it was hilarious. **(Flashback to November)** On the 3rd and 5th of November, we were intimate. **(Eye opener: Even our sexual encoun-ters were not genuine; it was all about control).** I am not trying to tally my sex life, but I am looking for God's promises to be fulfilled in my life. On another note, I stopped attending Bible Study on Tuesday morning at the church so that I can be available to him when ever he needed me. I seem to be doing everything under the sun for him to romance me. I wonder if I am really attractive to him, and I wonder if he is cheating on me as well. **(Eye opener: With Barry's seemingly psychological, spiritual, and other issues, I now realize that I was not the problem in our relation-ship; he was.)** The New Year, 2008, is approaching and I pray that God will change everything around for our good very soon.

RECAP OF EYE OPENERS IN 2007

In the year 2007, Barry continued to expose his true character. It was disclosed that Barry was addicted to taking the drug, oxycontin. This addiction was bad news because along with his addiction, he seemed to express a number of personality issues. Barry's love for trips continued at my expense. **It became obvious to me that he is a "user".** Secondly, he would not admit his real problem of having a possible ED; instead, he claimed that he suffered with back pain. Yet, he would mow the lawn, take long walks, and stand for hours in the kitchen cooking. He was an awesome actor who pretended to make me happy even sexually. **It was quite apparent that he had deceived me.** Thirdly, he thrived on being in the lime light as church musician and on programs in the community. He also sucked up the compliments of family members with a "big grin" when he cooked a delectable meal. To add to these, Barry stuck his chest out when relatives came around bragging about his computer knowledge. **He obviously has some "esteem issues".** Barry's fourth problem was holding onto grudges for years. He dislikes his mother and sister who live in our hometown. Additionally, he did not care too much for other family members and friends who live here either. Because he would not pray for forgiveness, God sees the sin of "unforgiveness" in his spirit; therefore God cannot heal or bless him. **Barry seemingly blocked and continues to block his own blessings because of his "unforgivable nature".** My husband would rather fight than love. We have had far more fights than love-making moments because of his built up anger against people.

Barry took full advantage of my submissive behavior which allowed him to control my resources and deportment and was the basis for me withdrawing from my investment funds and using my credit cards. Along with this issue, his other burdensome issue of being appreciated surfaced. How can this man show me appreciation when he has a deficit in this area? We must first value and love ourselves before we are able to value and love others. Still another issue is Barry's unforgiveness. As I stated earlier, God's laws are in effect when people harbor matters of the heart such as greed, unforgiveness, deceit, pride, disobedience, fear, jealousy, hate, and rebellion and the list goes on. God can not heal or allow us to prosper if our hearts are not pure. Only the pure in heart will reap the blessings. **It is my belief that Barry's "user", "deceit", "esteem", and "unforgiveness" issues are all psychological and are a result of his childhood experiences.**

I'm Still stuck in the Mud

(Chapter Four)

January 22, 2008—Dear Journal, I am not in a good mood today; I needed to visit my journal in order to vent. Quite a few things have occurred since my last visit. **(Flashback to funeral)** Barry's father made his transition from this life on January 5th. His home going celebration was on the 12th of this month. It is so strange that Barry was not going to attend his father's funeral until his sister who resides in New York along with my good friend convinced him to go. That sister along with his brother and nephew came for the funeral and stayed with us for about thirty hours. It was my first time meeting them, and we all got along very well. I really love them, and I was so glad to meet some of Barry's family members who he seems to be fond of and befriended. He seems to love this side of the family. Now, he is treating me really well, and I am feeling much better because of it. As I stated before, Barry is the kind of person that does not like many people for some reason or another. **(Eye opener: Barry knew how "to put on the charm" when his family members visited because he is an amazing actor. It is also possible that Barry's tolerance level was at its peak in light of the occasion.)**

The New Year is here already and my faith is much stronger due to TBN and the other Word channels. Tuning into these faith-based programs has helped me to press onward in our marriage. In addition to these programs, I have been reading Stormy O'Martin's book, *The Power of a Praying Wife*. This book has given me a so much hope. Even though I thought about "throwing in the towel" on my marriage, I have gained fresh insights about myself and Barry. Now, I prefer using what I have learned to salvage our relationship rather than give up on my husband. **(Eye opener: At that time, I was not aware that I could have tried every nugget of insight that I gained from both the faith-based programs and the book, but they would not have salvaged our marriage. Barry is in a category like no other man I have ever known; he truly needs help.)**

On January 26, Tyrese's friend, Bill, and his wife, Lisa, came into town to visit my son and his family. We invited them over to our house for dinner on Sunday evening. Since Lisa is a doctor, I asked her about the back pain shots verses taking medication to relieve chronic back pain. I explained to her that Barry didn't like taking shots and that his meds were not doing him any good. She stated that the shots were worth the pain to cure him several months at a time. I think Dr. Lisa's information went right over his head like a flock of dead ducks. I have cried out to God for help in this area, but there is not enough progress being made as far as he is concerned. Maybe, it will make sense to him that his wife needs fulfillment, and he will eventually decide to do something about it. At the moment, he cooks for me on a regular basis and is a little nicer to me, but these actions will never take the place of our intimacy. **(Awareness: Barry's lack of intimacy is seemingly psychological).** God has never failed me and I know that He did not bring me this far to leave me. I know that He will bring me out of this dilemma very soon. **(Eye opener: In God's timing, He brought me through this living hell to reveal Barry's true character).**

January 29, 2008 @ 8:00pm — Dear journal, since my last visit, I was a little down trodden but new life is in my relationship now. It makes me wonder if he is schizophrenic or something else because he gets into a good mood; then, he withdraws to himself for months at a time. **(Awareness: Even at that time, I had concluded that Barry appeared to be mentally unstable and had some issues).** I just don't get it with him. He has been romancing me in special ways lately, and I am loving it. I have to wonder if he is working on another trip at my expense, or maybe he wants me to purchase something for him. **(Awareness: I have concluded that he is a great actor and when he wanted something from me, he treated me very well).** Last Saturday, we had a nice, quiet intimate evening at home around the fire place about 9:00 p.m. We were actually intimately involved for the first time in a few months. I can't begin to say how much needed that was for me. I am looking forward to many more evenings like this one. How refreshing this experience was to me. He "acts" as if he loves me at times. Everyone tells us that we make a good couple, but they really do not know what's happening behind closed doors. **(Awareness: The key word is "acts". Barry is an accomplished actor who knows how to "turn on the charm", and he appears so genuine).**

January 30, 2008—Dear Journal, Today, we went "mall walking"; then, we rode around for a while. Barry is not one who engages in fun activities; he is just a routine type of guy. I like to explore different kinds of new activities such as a picnic in the park or just a short ride on the ferry. Brigitte and I have a little joke about him being "antiquated". Our son, Tyrese came over this morning and once again this evening. It looks like he and his wife are doing great in their relationship, and they seems very happy.

February 17, 2008—Dear Journal, Today, Barry's daughter from Atlanta came over to visit us. She told me about her mother's illness and her plans for her mother's arrival home from the hospital. I offered her some advice, but Barry became angry about this. He said that I should not get involved with that situation and that I was just like his sister that he hates so much. He told me that his sister tries to control his children at all cost and that it was not my task to give his daughter suggestions. In hindsight, I was just trying to be helpful, but he did not want me to help them at all. It is my belief that it is because of his hate towards their mother. He continues to chant the same old tune "She is getting what she deserves; I am not about to help her get assistance in any way." **(Eye opener: Barry is very vindictive and continues to harbor grudges against his own sister and former wives. His unforgiveness and bitterness towards others, particularly women, can be partly attributed to his lack of relationship with his own mother. Barry continues to block his own flow of love because he refuses to forgive others. This teaching is found in the book of Mark 11: 25-26 which states, "And whenever you stand praying, if you have anything against anyone, forgive him, that your Father in heaven may also forgive your trespasses. But if you do not forgive, neither will your Father in heaven forgive your trespasses." Barry's unforgiveness is sin and God's hands are tied in healing and blessing him. He really needs to repent of his sins by asking God to forgive him.)**

February 18, 2008 – Dear Journal, Today is President's Day. It is 7:10 am and is very somber outside. Since it rained most of the morning, we decided "to walk" around 1:10pm today. Barry was very quiet today as we walked. I really dreaded going with him today because I knew that he would be upset about the comments I made on yesterday. In knowing Barry's psyche, I knew that I needed to spend money on him in order to amend the hostility between us; for this reason, I treated him to lunch. Then, we went to Wal-Mart to buy a few groceries. We are alright now. Usually, when he gets upset with me, I would either send him to Sam's with my check card to buy some groceries or to any grocery store. As a result, he will begin to communicate and show more kindness towards me. He enjoys shopping for groceries and "eating in" when he cooks, or dining out at local restaurants when I treat him. **(Awareness: If I spent money on him, he would refrain from getting into one of his mood swings. Actually, I bought his affection.)**

Before the episode with his daughter, we were doing pretty well. We have had some intimate quality time twice so far this month. This is great considering last year. We only had sex six times last year and that was about two times every four months. I am praying for Barry's spirit to be healed as well as his body. His mind needs healing first. Unfortunately, he doesn't even realize it. I learned a long time ago that the mind controls and heals the body. I am continuing to pray that "the God of Abraham, Isaac and Jacob restore him to perfect health (mind, body and spirit); I know this is your will God". Barry plays in the church band but I never see him reading the *Word* of God and he is now saying that I focus on THE *WORD* TOO MUCH. He tells me, "Every time I look around you are talking about the *Word*". Then, he would say, "Don't you get tired of that." Barry is always telling me, "I need to give the *Word* a rest". I believe that if he became a student of the Bible, he would know that "God is a rewarder to those who diligently seek HIM". In other words, he should be praying about every situation that comes up against him instead of constantly worrying about what people have said about him and what they think and feel concerning him. I am always telling him not to concern himself about how they think or feel; if you know who you are, it should not matter anyway. **(Awareness: Barry seems to be self-conscious and a people pleaser. The enemy is a great deceiver and he is the father of lies. He gets into our minds by suggesting lies about ourselves, but we must know that the "Truth will set us free". Barry appears to have psychological baggage that seems to be a stumbling block in his Christian walk. Until Barry gets a closer relationship with our Creator, he is destined to remain an empty vessel that is full of mess and not God's *Word*.)** There is nothing on this earth greater than reading and acting on God's *Word*. It is the ONLY source that would give perfect PEACE. God please help me get this across to Barry.

March 2, 2008 on Sunday night about 10:49pm – Dear Journal, I intended to write more frequently in my journal, but I am always side tracked from entries on a daily basis. I am scheduled to have surgery on my right foot on the 14th of this month at 11:00 a.m. at the hospital. My foot continues to hurt because of my bone spur surgery. The doctor's prognosis is that my recovery period will be six weeks and that I will need a surgical shoe. I know I will be okay. Having this surgery will allow me more time to meditate on my circumstances. Barry is a good man to a certain extent but something about him seems a bit phony. **(Awareness: Even back in 2007, I felt that Barry was bogus).** I know I love my husband because if I did not, I would have left him by now. I realize that he is not where I am in Christ, and this is a big problem for me. **(Awareness: Barry is a baby Christian and I am a more mature Christian; we are unequally yoked).** I know that God is a God of change, and because of this, I will trust HIM for the VICTORY in my marriage. To help us get our victory, we went to church today. The title of the message was "Reaping What You Sow". Today's message blessed me so much. I realize that it is important to sow "Seed or Word" into my husband's life each day.

On the 14th of this month, I had foot surgery called (spur-nec-to-my); my 4th and 5th toes were treated as hammer toes. I am making first-rate progress with my surgery, and Barry has been wonderful with cooking and cleaning the house as well as doing the laundry. He is a decent husband in some areas, and I appreciate him for his assistance. Every day, I tell him that I appreciate what he is doing for me while I am recuperating. I have endeavored to make every effort towards encouraging Barry by telling him that he is the best husband that any woman could have. He does not know how aggravated I am about our intimacy because I would rather talk to God about it rather than confront him. **(Awareness: I held my peace about our lack of intimacy because I did not want an altercation with Barry. Our lack of intimacy seemed to be not only physical but also spiritual and psychological. Barry seems to need both spiritual and emotional healing.)**

March 23, 2008 – Dear Journal, Today is Easter Sunday. For the first time in years, I was unable to attend church, but at 5:00 a.m. this morning, Barry and I prayed together as we used to on Sunday mornings. It was good. He is very committed to Sunday morning prayer, and some Sundays, I pray with him. My preference is to pray out loud, but he prefers to sit and meditate for one hour. Most of the time, he falls asleep and snores. I wanted to pray out loud and read scripture, but he said that he did not want a *Bible* study. We just could not find common ground in this area, and for this reason, I allowed him to meditate. **(Awareness: Meditation is okay sometimes, but in Mark 11: 23-24, Jesus said, "...I say to you, whoever says to this mountain, 'Be removed and be cast into the sea,' "and does not doubt in his heart, but believes that those things he says will be done, he will have whatever he says, (and) ...whatever things you ask when you pray, believe that you receive tem, and you will have them. The Bible teaches the reality of faith's "confession" and that God's people have the ability to "speak to mountains" in our lives. God wants to change our vocabularies to line up with His *Word*. People of God should speak out faith, victory, and kingdom power with transparency, sincerity, and frankness.)** I love him, and I want us to grow closer to each other. I know that my prayers will eventually prevail.

March 26, 2008 @ 9:30pm – Dear Journal, God is answering my prayers. For the first time in weeks, we were intimate. Barry goes through so many changes during the course of a day to the point that it is tough to get his mind in the mood for intimacy. He is an angry, mean guy most of the time, and I have to think of nice things to do for him to bring him back into focus.

(Awareness: Barry had "tweaked me" or "knew my mindset"; therefore, he pretended to be angry and mean so that he could manipulate and use me). Sometimes, I really think he loves me, but he just does not know how to express his love towards me most of the time. He told me that he enjoys being with me and that if I ever decided to leave him, he was coming with me. That was a very sweet thing for him to say to me. He also told me that there were not enough hours in the day to spend with me and that we needed at least 30-40 hours together each day. These comments may have been made as a result of us praying together lately. I can see God manifesting Himself in our lives in a greater way. Barry asked me to pray for financial increase and for God to miraculously find ways to bless us; I also added that God will show us favor. *We are having the yard landscaped and we are putting an irrigation system planted into the yard which would cost us about $1,700 for the job to be done. It is a big sacrifice for us to do it, but it is so necessary. Barry asked me to pay half of the money to get the job done and I agreed to help him; I always do.* **(Eye opener: Now, I question Barry's kindness towards me. His compassion and sweet comments were vehicles used to seduce me to give him the funds he needed for the irrigation system in the yard.)** To add to this, *last year, he and I went to my tax accountant to have distributions drawn from my 401K plan each month to help with expenses at the house. We are flowing like married couples should right now, and it is good, but I always have to wonder if my husband is playing me for my assets. It seems as though he gets polite when he needs some money to do something or when we are about to take a trip.* **(Awareness: The only reason Barry seemed pleasant towards me was to use my investment funds. Also, he missed his calling because he has academy award winning qualities.)**

April 15, 2008 on Tuesday evening @ 5:15pm — Dear Journal, It is me again and I am feeling sort of melancholy right now. It has been four and a half weeks since my surgery. I am healing fairly well, but from time to time, I am feeling some strong pains resembling labor pains. It is okay because I am blessed to even have a foot. Barry has been wonderful throughout this entire ordeal and I can truly say that he has not slighted me the least bit. He has waited on me hand and foot, and I am grateful for having him service me. I have asked God to bless him in a special way, and I know he will. I see Barry as a very ambitious person who is always working in the yard, gardening, and planting vegetables. He is not weak in his deliverance with these things. He exerts the needed stamina or "goes full force" at all of his projects or hobbies. He also puts forth optimum effort in practicing his music for the church band. **(Eye opener: Barry's seemingly psychological or mental baggage from childhood interfered with him putting forth optimum effort with me and our mar-**

riage. We truly needed counseling). Another thing I have noticed about Barry is that he never allows our food supply to get low. He would remind me that we needed certain things. <u>Then, I will give him my check card to go shopping because he enjoyed shopping for groceries.</u> **(Awareness: Barry continued to deplete my funds)**. I usually cook our breakfast in the morning, but most days he would cook our dinner. <u>Shopping for groceries remedied our romance again. Barry has begun to compliment me again on my youthful look</u> although I am not feeling very youthful these days because we have not enjoyed any "connective activity" since my last visit. I will continue to ask God to speak to his mind. **(Awareness: When Barry depletes my funds by shopping or whatever, he shows kindness towards me. He is so superficial.)**

April 19, 2008 @ 6:30pm – Dear Journal, Nothing significant happened at home. Today was a day for me to reminisce. **(Flashback to last year's cruise)** I am reminiscing about our seven day cruise which was last year this time. It was an adventure for the two of us because we had never been on a cruise together. I had been on several cruises, but this was the first time that I had the distinct pleasure of a cruise with a man, especially my husband. For this unforgettable experience, we took some very nice pictures. I don't usually take good pictures, but this time I think that both of our pictures turned out great. To stay in shape, we exercised three to four times while we were on the cruise because there were countless varieties of scrumptious edible delights that we were not about to forego. As a matter of fact, we ate quite well. <u>I was disappointed the last night of the cruise because we had an argument over a bracelet that I bought him. I think he just wanted to get angry because it was stupid to cease conversing and enjoying each other's company because of such a simple thing like that. After the argument, we missed the Captain's Dinner the last night of our cruise, and we parted our separate ways. It is so ironic that during the entire seven days on the cruise, we were not sexually involved. He has issues; his actions made me feel extremely awful. To add to this drama, Barry continued being angry with me through customs and throughout our entire travel back home over something silly.</u> **(Awareness: Barry has extravagant taste and desires to experience the finer things of life at the expense of other people's money (OPM), but he has not discovered that these experiences are more enjoyable when they are spent with someone he truly loves and that someone returns that love. Love isn't love until you give it away. What a waste).**

May 9, 2008 on Friday morning about 11:15 am — Dear Journal, As I sit here under the hair dryer, I decided to write out my thoughts. For the last few days, I find myself getting back in a closer position with my husband. We seem to click with just about everything lately. I suggested that we count the money made from the garage sale that was inside of our money jar, and use it to buy a treadmill because ours is now worn out. He agreed and thought it was an excellent idea. We counted a few hundred dollars, went to Sam's, and purchased another treadmill today. Later today, we went to the hospital to visit a very sweet aunt on his father's side of the family. After we got home, I was totally surprised that we actually played around and had some fun together and it turned into quite an enjoyable evening. I know that my husband is capable of being complete with me, but he must stop working so hard on other projects and work hard on me. What he does around the house is important, and I appreciate him for this, but I need to be his "top priority" so that our lives could flow in the appropriate manner. **(Awareness: Being Barry's "top priority" never would have occurred because Barry did not even understand himself; in fact, he was all about himself and what he was able to drain out of me. Even now, he does not realize that he needs help.)** On the other hand, I am proud of the garden that he planted. This year, it has produced very juicy cucumbers, tomatoes, and bell peppers. I must admit that prior to planting the garden, Barry asked me to pray over the crop and it is producing quite well. In an effort to "beef up" the front yard by getting the grass tilted and sod laid along with the irrigation system, we would need to disburse $1,800.00. This is definitely needed because the grass is completely dead and needs rejuvenation. He seems to like having my support, especially financially. For this reason, I have been working with him on his projects around the house, **(Eye opener: Now, I realize that our marriage was all about what he could squeeze out of me. He continued to manipulate and use my resources.)**

May 15, 2008 on Thursday @ 3:30pm – Dear Journal, We attended Barry aunt's funeral on this past Saturday. Due to bad weather, his sister's flight from New York was cancelled, and she was unable to attend their aunt's funeral which is in a small town not far from Statesboro. By the time we got to the church in Sylvania, my feet were very swollen. As a consequence, we did not attend the burial. Instead, I treated him to dinner. **(Awareness: I continued to allow Barry to use and control me).** Then, we returned home and retired for the night. For the past few days we have been intimately involved. I don't know what came over him but I like it. **(Eye opener: Barry probably had a guilty conscience over using me so much. Usually, I would go out of my way to do any and everything to please Barry. He may have felt sorry for me. It is also possible that he is now taking some male enhancement drugs.)**

I'm Hurting inside, but I'm Still Shelling Out Cash

(Chapter Five)

May 15, 2008 @ 2:00pm—(Flashback to May 10) Since May 10, 2008, Barry has desired my affection. I was very pleased in receiving all this attention, but I needed to know the reason for the drastic change in his appetite; so, I asked him. He responded, "It is prayer." I know that I have been praying in season and out. He told me that he had been praying with me and without me, and I Bless God for that. He also commented that my new hair style with the curls turns him on. We are now drinking soy drinks as a replacement for a meal each day. This change in meal intake may have had an effect on his body. Whatever the reason, I know that God is still on the throne and I thank him for the sweet victory. **(Eye opener: It is my belief that Barry had begun using male enhancement drugs such as Viagra or Cialis for erectile dysfunction (ED); this makes more sense because soy drinks are mainly for women needing hormone replacement therapy HRT.)**

(Flashback to Mother's Day, May 11) On a happier note, Mother's Day was quite enjoyable. Barry cooked collard greens, pot roast, potato salad, glazed carrots, and rotisserie chicken. He gave me a bottle of Ralph Lauren cologne. Later that evening, Tyrese, Cheryln, and Brigitte came over for dinner and gave me two pairs of eye-catching Capri pants. Nique and her father sent me cards. I had several calls and well wishes for Mother's Day, and I have had a pretty good month, so far. We had a very pleasant time today. **(Eye opener: At times, it seems as though Barry is able to refrain from negativism.)**

Today (May 15), I had an appointment with my podiatrist. He stated that my foot is healing satisfactorily. To remove or lessen the scars, however, he prescribed a scar solution. My next appointment with my doctor is not until July of this year.

June 13, 2008—Today, my niece, Vera from Denver, came to visit us for another niece's graduation. She and I went for a massage after we ate lunch with Barry. Barry talked me out of going to my niece's graduation because he said that she did not come to visit us like a niece should; so, I didn't go. **(Eye opener: I allowed Barry to control my life. I should have attended my niece's graduation.)**

He cooked for my niece from Denver but refused to invite other family members over for dinner because he said that they did not deserve to come. I did not know what to say or do so I went along with that too for "peace sake". The menu was fried fish, cold slaw, and baked beans on Friday night; the only persons invited were our son and his family along with the niece from Denver. Barry is very selfish and likes to brag about his superior cooking skills. It is interesting to note that if a person rubs him the wrong way, that person would not be allowed to eat the food he had pre-pared. To ensure that he made you feel overlooked, he would put the word out that he had cooked a delicious meal and that you did not get invited to the party. **(Awareness: I continued to be controlled by Barry. He was very vindictive and seems to have a desire to hurt people, but he was only hurting himself because his heart was full of selfishness, spite, unforgiveness, and just plain evil. Any person's heart that is full of junk is really full of sin. God sees this sin in Barry's life; therefore, he seems to be blocking his own blessings.)**

June 14, 2008—On the day of my niece's graduation, we went to the res-taurant to see the family from out of town and in town, but we did not eat with them because of his attitude against my family members. I love my family and wanted to participate with what they were doing, but he has a great deal of hell in him. Later that day, my sister had a low country boil at her house for the graduate, and we went over for that. He was okay until my nephew asked him if he was treating me right. Barry replied, "He was". Then, my nephew said that he was just checking because he is aware of his tract record with divorcing his wives. Barry was very upset with him for making that comment and wanted to leave for home because my nephew had "struck a nerve". **(Awareness: Barry would not have been so upset if he had had civilized motives for his divorces. What happened was that Barry, once again, had to face himself and the reality of his past. This comment opened an old wound which he was desperately trying to cope with during our marriage. He knew within himself that he was his own worst enemy and that he probably created the disorientation in these marriages.)** While travelling home, Barry continued to discuss the comment which was made by my nephew. Actually, he was extremely bothered by my nephew's comment because it was the center of his conversation for many days.

June 21, 2008 Saturday —This weekend, we attended Barry daughter's graduation in Atlanta. While we were there, we visited some of my friends who had relocated to the Atlanta area and gave them some tomatoes from our garden. I sang a few songs while Barry accompanied me on the piano; we just had a wonderful fellowship with them. Next, we left their house and checked into the Hilton Hotel, changed clothes, and left to visit his daughter before going to a Braves game tonight. Our most enjoyable part of this event is that the Braves won the game.

June 22, 2008 Sunday— Barry gave his daughter a beautiful watch. I was surprised that he wanted to give her anything because he had been angry with her for not allowing him to walk her down the aisle on her wedding day. He talked very badly about her after she permitted her step father to walk her down the aisle. Anyway, I thank God that he was able to forgive her for that. **(Eye opener: At least, Barry was able to forgive his daughter, but to my knowledge, he still has not forgiven other loved ones. Barry's act of forgiveness could possibly have transpired because he was all about being seen. His actions could have been a ploy to be perceived differently. He is very concerned about people's perceptions and comments about him.)** Anyway, his daughter seems to be pleased with the watch that he gave to her. Her comments and gestures about her gift caused Barry to bask with delight. After her graduation, we took pictures with his daughter. Then, he wanted to show off in front of their mother by grabbing my hand when we walked off. He never holds my hand, so I know it was a show for her eyes to see. **(Awareness: Barry was at his best acting and trying to give reason for people to perceive his lies.)** Eventually, we left them and went to the Omni Hotel to eat dinner. The food was delicious, but to my disappointment later that night, I discovered that we were once again in the midst of a slump in being intimate. I know Satan is mad at us because we have the potential of having a great relationship and he knows that. We live very well, and we are stress free to a certain extent. Barry has relationship issues and is constantly pulling on me for financial assistance, but I do all that I can do for him with joy because I feel that one day, he will give it all back to me. At least that is my prayer. **(Eye opener: This is wishful thinking. That "day of Barry giving back to me" will never come. A person, who seems to manipulate and use others, is only concerned about themselves. Apparently, this kind of person does not have a conscience.)**

We are leaving for Denver next week. Barry has been pushing for us to take a trip to Denver for the longest. For this reason, I booked us a six day trip along with the children even though I knew that he would not help to finance this trip. We will leave on July 2nd. **(Awareness: Again, I used my funds to book another trip for us. He really, really used me. He has absolutely no principles. Most people would at least try to contribute towards a trip, but he didn't.)**

June 26, 2008 @ 6:10am Thursday—Today is a day of reminiscing on past events such as my niece's graduation and my other niece from Denver's visit. It is almost surreal how much I was manipulated by Barry.

July 9, 2008 @ 10:30am Wednesday—Dear Journal, It has been a while since I have visited you. We left for Denver on July 2nd and returned home on the 8th of July @ 2:00 a.m. We had a fairly good time. We were able to visit all of my family members, and I truly enjoyed them immensely. Tyrese and his family flew there with us. My funds were used for our flight, a rented Uplander, and lodging at the Hyatt Regency. Tyrese paid for his family's half but I paid for our part. **(Awareness: I was still "shelling out" cash, but I was very aware that he was and still is a user.)** We toured Investo Field, the Bronco's Stadium. The tour was very interesting, enjoyable, and informative. We also toured the mountains, the downtown malls, the 16th Street Mall, and several restaurants. After frequenting these restaurants, it was necessary for us to "work out" a few days at the hotel. On Sunday morning, Barry and I got into an argument about something silly; hence, he decided not to attend church. I was not about to allow his decision to affect my intention to attend church; so, I left him in the hotel room. This was very disappointing. It seems as though every time I expected him to do something with me, he would bow out with an argument. **(Awareness: When Barry did not want to do something, he will get into an argument to sever his obligation to participate. This was his way of "getting out of it". Instead, he should have told me that he was not interested in going so that he would not be perceived as a coward.)** We should be able to discuss these things as adults, but he acts so immature at times. I pray for him to grow more spiritually and to mature in his actions. I ask the Holy Spirit to arrest him and take control of his mind. He would rather fight than love and that is very sad. Although Barry did not attend church with me, church service was really fulfilling. The title of the message was "Help Is on the Way". I was greatly blessed by this message because Barry is an "up and down" person with mood swings. I never really know when he will explode in anger. The entire time we were in Denver, we did not connect at all and that is very pitiful to spend money like that and end up arguing over foolishness. We were intimate only once in June, and I am growing quite weary because he seems to be very sensitive and fragile about things. He retains feelings of hurt towards people and things. I believe it has a great deal to do with his childhood. Now, I am feeling as if I am too strong of a woman for him. I love him but he has many issues going on inside of himself. He gets angry over minute and insignificant things, and this bothers me a great deal. I am purposely trying to tone down my voice by speaking more softly in our conversations because he seems to think that I am raising my voice at him when I express myself about issues. Our son told me that he thinks that his dad feels as though I am "talking down" to him or that I consider him to be ignorant. This is not the case. He becomes intimidated when I use a broad vocabulary, but it is not intentional. I never intend any harm. Sometimes, certain words come out, and he gets angry with me about this. **(Eye opener: Barry may have issues of insecurity resulting from educational and childhood experiences.)** When I was employed, I encountered and mingled with a variety of people from diverse socio-economic backgrounds, and I was able to converse with them at their level of comprehension. I guess it has everything to do with my being single for such a long time. I sincerely feel that we needed a little more time of dating before we got married. Here I am locked into a big mess. **(Awareness: If we had taken more time in dating, I am assured that our true selves would have surfaced.)** He was not satisfied with just the six days that we spent in Denver so he asked me to book a trip to Denver for at least a month during the Christmas holidays. Even though I felt reluctant, I proceeded to book our tickets for this trip. Hopefully, things will get better between us. Everything is not bad between us but there are some very significant areas of our lives that need some serious adjustments.

July 16, 2008 @ 3:00pm— I am feeling depressed today. I can't seem to get over this past weekend's episode. I was feeling terrible about our trip to Denver, but on Friday night Tyrese, Cherlyn, and Brigitte brought some fish over to cook. We had a wonderful fellowship, and later that evening, Bri changed the screens on our cell phones. She put a heart on my phone and a dog house on his phone along with her picture on it. Then, he told her to take herself out and put me in the dog house, My feelings were hurt; so, I confronted him, but he denied it "big time". I try not to follow him up because I recognize the enemy's tactics. I later checked with Brigitte, and she also confirmed Barry's disheartening comment which was made about me. Well as always, I don't usually get an apology from him just maybe once, but not this time. He is becoming so disappointing to me. He is always complaining about something no matter what I do.

(Awareness: My belief is that Barry tried to make me feel unwanted as a tactic of retaliation because of his own insecurities.) When we first started seeing one another, he sent me flowers and complimented me about how good he thought I looked. Now, he cooks meals and sometimes brings me coffee in the morning. I appreciate him for these things, but I am not getting any physical love at all. We seem to be fighting, fighting, and fighting all the time. My heart is broken. **(Awareness: Barry seem to be suffering inside because of so many seemingly psychological issues—esteem and needing to be appreciated; insecurity around me and needing to seek revenge; malice toward his mother and sister and not wanting to be around them; meanness towards my family members and showing them spite by not inviting them for dinner, and unforgiveness and grudges against his own children. His mind had become so bottled up with all this negative stuff that he fought with the person closest to him which is me, his wife. I can not recall Barry asking for forgiveness for any of these things. It is my belief that had he asked God for forgiveness, God would have revealed how he could help himself. At this point, it will take a miracle to help Barry. Yet, God is a God of "Grace and Mercy" and will forgive us seven times seventy.)**

July 19, 2008—We went to North Carolina for my extended family reunion. We met many of my mother's family members. On Friday and Saturday night, we were guests at a nice hotel sponsored by me, of course. **(Awareness: I was still using my funds for trips.)** All and all, we really enjoyed the camaraderie with family members. On Sunday after church, we left to visit his daughter in Greensboro. When we arrived, she was busy, and in view of this, we checked into the hotel and got something to eat. He became upset with his daughter because he said that she knew that we were coming, but she was too busy for us. He said that he was never going back there again even though she and her husband rode us around that evening when they got home. **(Awareness: As I stated earlier, Barry was like a grenade—if you touched his feelings negatively, he would explode.)** When we returned home on the 21st, we rested for a few days. After that, we celebrated Barry's birthday at Outback restaurant with Tyrese and his family. They gave him a very nice fleece jacket and a brown pair of tennis shoes.

August 10, 2008 — I celebrated my birthday at Masato's with several family members and friends. We had a great time. My girlfriend gave me a gift certificate to Red Lobster; Tyrese and Cherlyn gave me a gift certificate to Macy's, and Barry gave me some perfume. We had a very pleasurable day.

Since our return from Denver, Barry continues to mention his need for a change of scenery. He hounds me about booking a trip to "hang out" in Denver for an entire month. His point is that a trip could possibly be therapy to help him to feel better about life. I ignored him for a long time, but he is very persistent about taking a trip to Denver to experience the snow. **(Awareness)** Something in my spirit did not want me to do it, but I decided to give it one last chance; I succumbed to his requests and booked the trip to Denver during the Christmas and New Year holidays. **(Awareness: We need to obey our spirit because it forewarns us of dangers ahead.)**

August 30, 2008— A cousin from our extended family in North Carolina came to visit us for a few days. We weren't expecting them to stay quite as long, and as a consequence, Barry became very upset with them and forced them to leave by keeping the house hot. I thought that what he did was cruel, but that was and still is his mindset. Instead of doing this to them, he should have told them the truth. After all, Barry was the one who invited them to come. Initially, he was very gracious and kind to them. Afterward, he decided that they were staying around too long and changed his kindness to meanness. **(Eye opener: Barry was very temperamental and easily offended. If you slighted him one way or another, he would seek vengeance upon you. He really should have been honest about this issue and confronted this couple. The *Word* says, "Vengeance in the Lord's, he will repay." In hindsight, I should have shared this concern with this couple before Barry handled this situation, but I had become so controlled in this relationship that I allowed him to do this.)**

September 5, 2008 @1:12 pm— It has been a while since I have visited with you. I am anxious about this visit today due to an update of events. Since my last visit, we have had some falling out, of course, but the one that is most recent is when I forgot to give him the $400.00 per month that I usually give him. **(Eye opener: Barry's major concern was to receive my monthly disbursement.)** He just went crazy on me. I told him that it was just an oversight and that all he had to do was to remind me. Our relationship has been really bad for a few days. He blew this incident up to be a "big thing". So, as always, I asked him if we could talk about it; so, we both had an opportunity to vent. His venting became arguing instead of conversing with me. He does not know how to hold a conversation; he argues. In my opinion, he cannot hold a calm conversation with me. I am shocked that he would shut everything down because of something like this. **(Eye opener: In retrospect I am able to perceive that Barry is indeed money driven. When his finances are not "in place", he becomes threatened with insecurity. Acquiring money makes him happy. He loves to have money. We all know that "the love of money is the root of all evil".** He is indeed a mad man. I addition to his money driven attitude, I think that some his madness may also be accredited to his chronic back pain which may contribute to his sexual inactivity; this could be a reason for him being excessively cranky. Only God knows the real truth about this madness. I do wonder why he snaps at me. In August, we had four encounters which were better than our first year or two together. I know he is a sick man mentally, physically, and spiritually; so, I am continuing to pray for his mind, body and spirit. This man has lot of issues going on with him, and he holds onto every hurt or harm he feels has ever been done to him. He allows these issues to block out his personal pleasures in life... I call it having a one tract mind that is "trapped in a shell of negativism". Once he learns that no matter what happens, the JOY OF THE LORD would be his strength. Then, he would have conquered what life is all about. **(Eye opener: Barry continued with his temper tantrums, but it was and still is seemingly because of a combination of all the negative stuff in his mind that has ultimately affected him physically. According to scripture, only a transformed mind filled with God's precious promises can saturate his heart and change Barry into a new man. Romans 12:1-2)** In spite of all of his mess, I keep "moving on to the high call of Christ Jesus".

October 4, 2008 @1:18pm— I have not visited my journal in a while, but today, I opened up my old computer, went into my old work data, and discovered that I may have $30,000 of retirement funds that may not have been disbursed as of yet. Barry was so excited when I told him this information that even before I checked it out, **he had begun planning a cruise (WOW).** I proceeded to contact the company which took my information, investigated the situation, and called me once a week for about four weeks. Barry was sweet to me during this period and was not upset with me about anything. Now, I wonder if he is for real or fake with me. He talked with the company himself telling them that his wife is getting stressed out about them taking so long to locate the funds. He told them that it would be considered an urgent matter at this point. **(Awareness: As long as there was an opportunity to retrieve funds, Barry the actor would surface; he never became upset. Obviously, he seems to be able to control his temper when he felt that he would receive some monetary or other rewards. Barry vehemently pursued the seeming disbursement of my funds. He allowed his user mentality to surface without any shame.)** Within two days after his conversation with the company, this scenario ended. The company contacted us and stated that the funds had already been disbursed with the 401k funds. Barry was so disappointed, and from that moment on, he went back to being himself again. **(Awareness: Barry was extremely upset because he wanted to use me once again, but he couldn't.)**

October 6, 2008 @ 2:00am—It is early morning, and I cannot sleep. My spirit is not settled, and in view of this, I decided to sit in the family room and write about my life. My life is very dull at this very moment, and it has been for while. It is like a roller coaster, and I am screaming for it to stop to let me out. But the God in me keeps me rooted and grounded and faithful to the vows that I promised when I married Barry. I keep thinking about "for better or worse, richer or poorer, sickness and in health until death do us apart." A few days ago the company that I used to work for deposited a check into my account for $500.00. The next day the phone company sent me a gift card for $100.00. Three days later, I received another check for $3,700.00 from another company. Barry' entire demeanor changed; he became attentive and sweet towards me again, and I know it was because of the money. He is money driven, and I am emotionally ruled. I have "20/20 vision" on him right now, but I still want to help him to walk in righteousness and forsake wrong doing. I rely on the WORD to guide me, and I am trying to set an example for Barry to let a pure light shine and to get real with God. Philippians 4:19 says that "God will supply all of our needs according to His riches in Glory by Christ Jesus". It does not state that man will supply our needs. I believe that God is using me to show him that he is a faithful to those who LOVE HIM. We are doing well again, and we are intimate once again. **(Awareness: Maybe, our intimacy is a result of my new found monetary rewards. He always gets "chummy when I get money".)** On the contrary, there is a downside to our moment of joy; we are both experiencing physical challenges. I have tendonitis bursitis in my right shoulder. Because of the excruciating pain, I set up an appointment with my doctor yesterday. She prescribed three medications to repair this problem. Along with God always being the great physician, I am confident that these medications will get me back on tract again. Barry is also still in pain, but I am looking for the day that he will become violent about his healing according to Matt. 11:12. **(Awareness: This was wishful thinking. Barry's inattentiveness to reading God's *Word* nullifies his relationship with God. Reading the Bible has medicinal benefits. A violent believer would be passionate about reading and acting on the precious promises of God so that he could receive his physical, mental, financial, or spiritual healing.)** A pleasant note is that next weekend we are going to Atlanta for the Falcons and Chicago Bears' game. My sister and her husband are coming with us. On my next journal visit, I will update you on the trip.

October 19, 2008 @ 3:45pm Sunday evening—Dear Journal, We went to Atlanta on the 11th of October and returned on the 13th. The Falcons won the game and we had a fantastic time. We stayed at the Marriott Marquis Hotel. The breakfast menu was awesome, and the hotel was five star quality. My shoulder was paining me the entire time that I was there, but I persevered. Of course, Barry was in pain as well. I do not allow pain to control me so I just spoke word over my body while in pain. Barry, on the other hand, continues to speak negative words such as "I am hurting", and relies on the medication (oxycontin) to relieve his pain. We were surrounded by beauty but did not enjoy each other intimately as always.

When we returned home, <u>Barry created an argument over an email that</u> <u>I received from my nephew. His anger towards me was ridiculous. He</u> <u>did not speak to me for several days. It is my belief that he did it to steal</u> <u>away from home for a while, and he did.</u> He allows the devil to jump inside of him during our trips and right after our trips. <u>This time, the Holy Spirit</u> <u>ministered to my spirit and said that it was about him being angry with</u> <u>himself for a lack of performance. He gets angry with me about his pain</u> <u>and inability to become intimate when we travel.</u> **(Awareness: Being in chronic pain and drumming up disagreements had become Barry's coping mechanisms in handling his ED problem.)** I truly believe that his medicine is making matters worse than better.

In Sunday school this morning, one of the ladies suggested that I write my concerns down so that my vision for Barry will be made manifest. <u>I</u> <u>told her that I am always journaling positive words from God over him.</u> **My prayer is "Today, Lord I pray for Barry's complete salvation, and I ask you to call him into completeness where he will serve you in spirit and in truth. Cause him to sell out to you and give his heart totally to you. Then, his eyes and ears will open for instructions ONLY from YOU GOD. Heal his BODY, MIND AND SPIRIT!!! No one can intercede but you God. Lord, also look inside my life and take over. Bless every area of our lives and make us ONE again. I claim healing for both of us and rebuke the enemy in Jesus' name."**

November 3, 2008 @ 12:35am—Dear Journal, Just about every week we are having a disagreement of some kind over very trivial things; this episode was about my left eye jumping. It is all craziness; he just can't get past the drama. I do not understand this man. I asked him about twenty minutes ago "When am I going to get my husband back?" He responded with" when I start to act like a wife and stop treating him like a child." I really feel abused because I have supported him through thick and thin. When we are in bed, most of the time, he never touches me. <u>It has been over a</u> <u>month and we have not been intimate</u>. His mind wavers when things are not "floating" the way he expects them to. <u>He argues, pouts, and becomes</u> <u>extremely selfish to the point where he denies me in the marital bed. I am</u> <u>miserable, and he really does not care.</u> This past weekend, we went to the homecoming game for the high school in our neighborhood. I left the house to purchase two high back chairs for us. It is so sad to know that a few days ago, I suggested that he purchase some chairs for the game if he wanted me to go with him, but he was "too cheap" to do so. *If there* *was anything that I wanted or needed, I would need to buy it for myself* *because he was too cheap to get it. I feel as if I have a room mate instead* *of a husband.* <u>I can't even remember the last time Barry bought something</u> <u>for me</u>. I pull a lot of weight around here; <u>I pay the utilities, the telephone</u> <u>bill, life, car, and dental insurance. In addition to these, my contribution</u>

of $200.00 a month goes towards grocery expenses. This totals about $919.00 per month. In addition to these items, when we go on trips, I usually pay for lodging and all of our meals. When we go out to dinner in town, I am the one who's "shelling out the cash". On our vacation trip to Denver, I used my sky miles for airfare, rented the SUV, and paid for a six night stay at the Hyatt Regency. While we were in Denver, Barry's only contribution towards our expenses was taking the check for a few dinners; he did not offer to buy me one thing while we were there. I have never burdened or saddled him with any responsibility for me. In fact, he is my husband, but I am spending all my money. Yes, he cooks most of the meals at home, but this is not every day and I share in the cooking. I wait on him hand and foot. For example, I prepare and serve him meals in the family room or in the bedroom. I respond to his requests to get items from the kitchen, and I most certainly keep the house immaculate to the point where he brags about it to other people. To top all of these, Barry never has to worry about having clean clothes to wear because I take care of these as well. Yet, he has the nerve to say, "You are not being a good wife." **(Awareness: It is obvious to me that Barry is a manipulator, user, and abuser. His actions have led me to believe that he did not care about me; his major focus in our marriage was to squeeze what he could out of me and drain me dry. Even when he knew that I desired attention, he refused to accommodate me. I made enumerable deposits into his life, but I received exceedingly scarce returns. I allowed Barry to use and abuse me to the point that my life with Barry had become almost unbearable, a living hell.)**

Love Don't Cost a Thing

(Chapter Six)

I have laid hands on this man so many times for his healing, but he just pretends to receive from God. When his pain gets bad, I encourage him, and I am always supporting his music ministry. For his comfort and peace of mind, I bought us a GPS, a wireless air card for the internet, and a high back executive chair for the desk top. I bought him jewelry, lots of black underwear, clothes such as shorts, pajamas, sweaters, and shirts and special shoes from foot smart to support his back. Every time I get some extra money such as gifts or surprises, I share it with him. The last time it was $500.00, and it is recorded in my checkbook. I probably have given him about $3,000.00 in cash outside of the $919.00 per month, household expenses, and the many trips we had taken this year. There are so many nice things that I tried to do for my husband, yet he and I are growing apart. **(Awareness: I continued to allow him to manipulate, control, and use me. I had learned my lesson, but I continued to submit to him in faith. I realize that I can not buy love.)** I just don't know what else to do so I am going "cold turkey" for a while. He does not appreciate me at all and that is very disappointing to me because I have tried to do my best by him. I may not be everything a man wants, but I am surely not a bad catch at all. I believe there is someone out there who would appreciate someone like me. I have a kind heart, and I love very hard to please my mate. **(Eye opener: It is not so wise to reveal the extent of your love for someone; your lover will seem smothered and lose respect for you.) Prayer time**—"God show your face strong and show me what to do next. I have been sensitive to my husband's needs and have showed him love, tenderness, and a kind spirit. I am assured that deep down in his soul he knows that I am a very decent person and a fine wife to him. I admit that I am not perfect and have faults, but for the most part, my good qualities outweigh my bad ones."

November 3, 2008 @ 2:00 pm—Dear Journal, I wish I could feel better, but depression keeps overwhelming me today. It is one of those sad dreary days outside that makes it even worse. Barry adores the rain, but I sometimes wonder why he never uses it as an opportunity to romance me. Rainy days should be used for us to become closer in our relationship, especially, if we are married and at home. Love is only what you make of it, but my husband would rather FIGHT than LOVE. I have been a humble wife due to Barry's back pain, but it has to be because of his selfishness that he does not pursue me. It is interesting that he only pursues me when I am doing something special like taking him on a trip, giving him some money, buying him something, or paying the bills. His actions are inexcusable and noticeable at this point and time in my life. I don't believe he adores me anymore; he is so dry towards me most of the time. He used to tell me that I was pretty and that I look good. All of that kind of talk is limited now unless he is trying to butter me up. **(Awareness: Barry continues to use his charm to manipulate, use and abuse my kindness and resources.)** I cannot express enough how these things are affecting my life. I realize that I am responsible for my own happiness and I try to be, but I look for my husband to bring some of that happiness to me as well. I am not going to talk to him a great deal anymore and maybe we will get along better. Although I am a talker and enjoy conversations with various people, he seems to want me to be very quiet and not even to talk on the telephone with my friends and family too much. **(Eye opener: My family and friends might have helped to pull the covers off of Barry so that I could see him for who he truly is.)** I think this is crazy, but I will pull back a little and see what happens.

November 14, 2008 @ 3:00pm—Dear Journal, (Flashback) On Thursday, November 6, Barry had his wisdom tooth extracted and was in great pain. **(Flashback)** Last Friday, November 7, he felt better after I pampered him back to recovery. We laughed and enjoyed the evening together. In a telephone conversation, we spoke with his sister from New York; she told us that she was happy that we were getting along. We had a good union in the spirit. **(Flashback)** On Saturday morning, I got up and prepared a sausage and egg breakfast; then, I left to get my hair curled. At breakfast about 10:45am, he stated that our dental hygienist and her son were coming over for piano lessons today. Immediately, I asked him when was he going to inform me, and he said that he had forgotten to tell me that they were coming over. **(Awareness: As always, I went on with what I had to do and said no more about it to him. I personally feel that he disrespected me in regards to that, but I brushed it off just to try to get along with him.)** This same thing happened on November 1ˢᵗ when his nurse from the doctor's office and her daughter came over to the house when I was gone. He stated that she brought her daughter over for piano lessons. He isn't right by any means for doing this**, (Awareness: I have perceived that there is obviously some affinity towards those women for him to do this to me.)** I think that he wants me out of his life but does not know how to tell me because when we were newlyweds, he insisted that I look in his eyes to promise that I will never leave him. Likewise, he told me that he will never leave me. I am aware of Satan's devices; he comes like a thief in the night to steal, kill, and to destroy (John 10:10). **(Awareness: It is a known fact that hurting people hurt people. He is hurting from his previous relationships with his daughters, his sister who is in town, his mother, and previous other hurtful events and things he has discussed with me. It is as if he has transferred all of his "baggage" into our relationship.** I believe that Joyce Meyers calls it "baggage". **Unfortunately, for years, it has been a way of life for him, and he just can't turn it a loose. He must not recognize that I am indeed a blessing to him and want to help him heal from his past.** He is indeed a mad man from time to time. We cannot have a decent conversation without his argumentative tone of voice.)** I told him about it, but he continues to use a fussy tone of voice when we discuss our relationship. Now, I assume that something is going on with him and someone else because he shows no sign as being interested in me as his wife. He is just bearing with me for my support financially and to enjoy pleasurable events. He knows that he would not have a social life if it were not for me. I do not regret the support that I have been to him because I truly love him and trust God to change him. What I regret is that I did not listen to our son before I married him. He was so right that his dad and I are two different people. **(Awareness: I jumped into this marriage without really knowing that he was saved and sold out to God as I am. He is a GREAT ACTOR and made me believe that he was sold out to God. I just know things would have been different had I taken more than a year to get to know him once again, but he was so pushy and forceful, and I fell right into it.**

We have had some very silly arguments such as using his shampoo (even when he shaved his head bald). When he grew his hair back, his shampoo was in my bathroom and he was angry because he said that I should have put it back. Believe it or not, this caused us not to speak for four days, and he was actually very bitter. This was so stupid to me but to him, he was justified for getting angry. **(Awareness: A saved man "sold out to God kind of man" would have handled it so differently. I told him that his actions were foolish, and it makes me think that it really was not about the shampoo at all and that it was about something else.)**

November 17, 2008 @ 11:30am—Dear Journal, On Monday night we had a chat about our relationship. He asked me if I wanted a divorce, and

I responded, "If you do, it would be fine." On Tuesday November 18, he apologized about his actions, and I accepted. Now, he is trying to act a little better with me. He is hugging and kissing me again, and it feels very strange to me because he had not done that in a long time. He is also telling me that he loves me. **(Awareness) I really do not know what to make of this right now.)**

November 18, 2008 –Dear Journal, He helped me clean the house for Thanksgiving, and I decorated the house as I always do at the beginning of the autumn season. I discovered that his sister from New York is coming to visit us for the holidays, Barry totally flipped the script and was again kind to me. **(Awareness: This is why he was acting better with me so that I could help him entertain his sister. It is always a motive for his niceness towards me.)**

November 22, 2008 on Saturday morning — Dear Journal, We picked up Barry's sister from the airport, and **I treated both of them to breakfast at Cracker Barrel.** **(Awareness: Once again, I am paying the expenses; his reason for being amiable towards me was to use my resources during his sister's visit.)** She is a nice person, and I really like her. Prior to her arrival, she and I had been talking over the telephone for a while, and she said that I was the only wife of his that she has ever liked or has even taken a risk to stay in the same house with. She knew his girl's mothers and his last wife who assumed that she was Barry's woman. After finishing breakfast, we arrived home. Once she had unpacked her bags and taken a short break, around ten o'clock, we left the house to sightsee the city.

The children came over that evening, and we feasted on a low country boil. The food was delicious and everyone enjoyed the fellowship. She and I have spoken about her brother over the phone several times and she knows how he is. I have shared many subjects with his sister and I let her know that he gets angry over so many little things. She understands that he has a problem getting along with women. On Sunday, we attended church, and we had an eventful week except Barry lashes out at me sometimes. **(Awareness: Most of the time, I ignore him because I know that he is quite immature. Sometimes, I defend myself if it becomes overbearing.)**

November 27, 2008 – Dear Journal, Our Thanksgiving dinner guests were his sister, his daughter and her husband and their four children from Carolina; our son Tyrese, his wife Cherlyn, and their daughter Brigitte, and my other granddaughter Nique. We had a total of thirteen guests at our dinner table for Thanksgiving. We played games like "picturenaire", and reminisced about other pleasurable times. Thanksgiving was GREAT! I wish I could replay it! The food was scrumptious, and kindred spirits were phenomenal. This was one of my most pleasurable Thanksgiving experiences. <u>Since Thanksgiving, we have been intimately involved twice during that week. (WOW)!!!</u> **(Awareness: <u>His actions have revealed that his mind is distorted and that he can do what he tells his mind to do. He is just stubborn and FULL OF HELLISHNESS. Barry enjoys a good falling out once or twice a month; then, he uses it as a reason not to become connected as a married couple should.</u> (Eye opener: It is possible that these disagreements were staged because he was incapable of handling more sexual activity.)** This is very weird because we are married and instead of enjoying all of the pleasures in life, he finds reasons not to. <u>I must say that when we are intimate, he seems to enjoy it very much.</u>

December 1, 2008—Dear Journal, This evening, Barry and I went to America's Best to fill his eyeglass prescription. While we were there, we discovered that the eyeglass technician had just recently moved to this area from New York and had not found a church home, as of yet, that does not require "upscale dressing up". She also told us that her husband does not like to wear suits. <u>I informed her that at our church, you "come as you are", or she could wear something like what she had on if she wanted to. At the end of our little talk, Barry invited the technician to visit our church.</u>

December 2, 2008—Dear Journal, I am so confused about today. While we were mall walking, it was very quiet due to the episode that occurred last night. <u>Barry brought up the encounter with the technician again and stated that I had addressed the young lady wrong by saying "she could wear what she had on to church."</u> When I said it, she seemed to have understood, and she said okay. He blew it all out of proportion and was angry with me about this comment. If I were not a Christian, I would cuss not curse right now because he is so ignorant and crazy with his thinking. **(Awareness: Here again, it is a reason to become angry with me until he finds something else. He made some very sarcastic remarks to me about that incident. I stopped walking with him and went downstairs in the mall to finish my walk.)**

December 5, 2008 @ 5:00pm—Dear Journal, I reminisced about his sister's visit and Thanksgiving with our children.

December 6, 2008 – Dear Journal, Today is my mother's birthday and Barry is angry with me about last night. He left the house several times today without speaking to me and he is still not speaking to me. I asked him for the plumber's phone number to give to a friend; he gave it to me and kept right on going without saying a word to me. I tried to create small talk with him by telling him about the towel rack in the bathroom being broken and telling him that the children said that they were coming over tonight. He told me that he did not know about the children coming over that night. Then, he asked me for the air card for the internet. That was the end of that conversation. My husband is a very mean and hateful person, and I can't believe that I did not discern this spirit when he came back into my life. I sincerely felt as if he was a different man as I had become a totally different kind of woman since our teen years. (Awareness: On the contrary, **he seems to be the same old grouchy, mean, and unstable man that he was when he was younger.**) The only difference is that he has become a much better actor this time around in life because he certainly fooled my "socks off". He made me believe that he was filled with the HOLY SPIRIT. He actually went so far as speaking in tongues. (Awareness: **How can he play around with God like this? Is it possible for him to go to HELL for this? Maybe I should not judge him, but he is wrong for doing this to me. This is puzzling. WHERE DID I GO WRONG?**)

Barry remained angry for several days to the point that I was very tempted to cancel our previously arranged trip to Colorado. We were scheduled to leave on December 12 because we had planned our trip there for at least a month. He had been pushing me to book this trip because he had not experienced "snow". A few days later, he adjusted his attitude by "buttering me up", apologizing, hugging and kissing me, and saying that he wanted our marriage to work, and that he would do anything to make it work. (Awareness: Barry knew that he needed me in order for him to visit Denver; therefore, he "put the charm on me extra strong" so that he could make this trip. As you can see, he had the ability to change his demeanor to get what he wanted. Also, he would say or do anything to "have his way".

December 12, 2008—Dear Journal, When we arrived at the Denver Airport, it was a cold night, and the snow covered the ground. Barry was like a little kid, extremely excited about the snow. He told me several times that he had never been in a "real snowy city" where the snow lingered on the ground for days at a time. Even though Barry had wronged me, used me, and abused me, I wanted to give him that experience, because he practically begged me for this trip. My niece picked us up from the airport. Initially, we had booked a room at a local hotel, (Awareness: I was not about to "put out" cash for our airfare and hotel accommodations on another trip and allow him to, once again, relinquish his responsibility totally upon me.) When I expressed this concern to my niece, she invited us to reside at her house. We slept in the bedroom downstairs. It was as if we had our own apartment because it was very private. We had everything that we needed down there except for the kitchen. On Saturday morning while we lounged around the house and ate breakfast, my niece, a self-employed day care proprietor, went to her business to attend to some unfinished paperwork. Barry went outside to play in the snow. Later that day, Barry prepared Italian sausage for lunch. My sister, my nieces' mother and her husband were visiting Denver from Texas, and they were invited over to eat lunch with us. We enjoyed their company immensely during their short visit. The next day, she and her husband returned to Texas. That Saturday night, my niece invited us to a Christmas party. When she arrived home from work that evening, we dressed for the Georgia Club's Party at the condo's clubhouse. We socialized and ate with her friends and some other family members until about 12:30 am. While we were there, it started to snow again about 10:00 pm. Barry went outside to walk in it while my niece gave him some pointers on how to properly walk in the snow. He did well. The next day which was Sunday, we attended church with my niece. <u>The preacher's message was "Changing Addresses" which was quite appropriate for Barry because it was emphasizing the point "If You Do What You Have Always Done, You Will Get What You Have Always Gotten."</u> **(Awareness: I thought that it was a "right on" message for Barry.) (Eye opener: Change isn't change until we change. Barry is capable of changing through the help of the Holy Spirit. This could only occur if he established a relationship with the Lord by "hanging out' with him—read the word, attend Bible study, fellowship with believers, and pray daily. If he did these things, his empty void would be filled and his mind would not be conformed to the world. Instead, he would be transformed by a renewed mind. It is a process to surrender oneself totally to God, but it will occur. Later on, it will be revealed that Barry's demeanor was totally "in check" as long as he was using the resources of my family members. <u>Keep in mind that Barry only controlled his behavior with "will power" which he could eventually loose, but if he possessed a renewed mind, both his heart and behavior would change, resulting in positive character that never changes)</u>**. The message was excellent and the choir sang well also.

We drove separately so that my niece could handle her business after church on Sunday. She is a business woman, and we did not want to hinder her progress. We left church and went to Ruby Tuesday for pot pie and a salad; it was very cold that day. We left there, and went to Circuit City to take the GPS which had stopped working that day. The service reps exchanged it for a new one because it was under warranty. For dinner that night, we met my niece and her boyfriend. He treated us to an Indian dinner. He is Iranian, and he introduced us to his favorite restaurant. The food was tasty, and we had a very good time. By the way, this was our second Sunday there. On our first Sunday in Denver, we did not attend church. Instead, we stayed home all day because my niece had scheduled a photo session at her home for the family members to come over to take pictures. We had a pleasurable time with family members, and I was so grateful to see them. He cooked a large pot of chili and a large pan of corn bread. It was so delicious that all of it was eaten. Even the two female photographers ate with us. **(Awareness: Barry always likes to show everyone that he can cook.)**

December 15, 2008 – Dear Journal, We called my nephew to take us to the grocery store, and that was when he insisted that we use his car. This was surely another blessing through my family. My nephew's mother and her husband used the car while they were there, and when they left, he offered his car to us. He told us that all we had to do was to take care of his car, pay the insurance on the car for one month, and drive the car for as long as we needed. On Wednesday night, I wanted to attend a Bible Study at Heritage Christian Center ("HCC") in Aurora, Colorado. This is a church that I have visited several times during my many years of vacationing in Denver. HCC was not there when I lived in Denver during the 80's, but whenever I went to Denver to visit my sister in the 90's, she would always take me to HCC Church along with her, and I would thoroughly enjoy it. The service was just as I had expected it to be; it was a very informative Bible study, and the choir sang out of the city of their souls. It was so spirit-filled to both of us that we decided to go back on Saturday for their Christmas play at 2:00 pm. The play was entitled "What a Wonderful World". It was a beautiful experience and the characters played their roles very well. After we left the play that evening, another niece who came to watch the play with us took us to Red Lobster for dinner. Following dinner, we rode all over Denver sightseeing that day and every day thereafter. There are several new developments that are just breathtaking. I cooked breakfast for us every day except for when we went to the Village Inn one morning. Most of the time while we were in Denver, we ate dinner at the restaurants such as the Golden Wok, First City Grill, Old Chicago, Fitzgerald's, Juicy Lucy, Pizza, Wing Stop, Ruby Tuesday and other restaurants. On one occasion, Barry cooked some shrimp gumbo, collard greens, black eyed peas and some ham while we were there also. He invited Denise, my incarcerated nephew's wife, out to dinner with us and she treated us. The next time we went out, Barry suggested that we go get her because he felt that she was sad and lonely; so, I said okay. On the third time, he suggested that she come with us, I thought it was a bit strange that he kept asking for her to come along. He brainwashed me to believe that the rest of the family had abandoned her so we should show her some love. I bought into his idea of love because I am all about love and unity. **(Eye Opener: It is not a good idea to have another woman (relative, friend, or stranger) to string along on any date with you and your husband. I was naïve in allowing Denise to accompany us on**

our outings. The question to ask is "How would he have reacted had I invited one of his male in-laws on a date with us?" Even though we have had our share of challenges and differences, Barry would not have liked it one bit. If it's good for the rooster, it's good for the hens.) We looked at a few town homes because suddenly, Barry wanted to move to Denver after having been there a few weeks. He told me that he adored this part of the country. He kept telling me, "I am moving to Denver". He was so anxious to move there that he went to a bank in downtown Aurora and spoke with a loan officer; he was pre-approved to buy some property there. As for me, I really love Denver and I wouldn't mind living there, but Barry seems to have too many mood swings and psychological issues for me to trust that kind of move. As we were touring the city, we seemed to get lost, and, of course, he blamed me and argued with me. **(Awareness: He got over it very quickly. After all, he knew that he was at the mercy of living in my niece's house and using my nephew's car. I have never seen Barry pull himself together so quickly.)** I was laughing on the inside because I knew that he usually remains angry for at least 3-4 days, but most times, it will last for a week or more before he recovers from that angry spirit inside of him. He demonstrated that he was able to get himself together much more quickly than he had previously. **(Awareness: Barry's anger episodes were controllable and he proved it. On another occasion during our visit, he left me at the house and went to my niece's daycare to wash her vehicle. He had been gone for about three and a half hours or more**. I thought that this was a long time to wash a vehicle, but I did not say anything to him. When he came back to the house, he told me that her vehicle was filthy, and it took hours to clean it. Later that day, Denise informed me that Uncle Barry stopped by her house. I asked him "Why didn't you tell me that you were going to her house?" He responded, "I went to take her some Trim-Max tea." **(Awareness: His answer was a big, big lie from the pit of hell. Denise lived about 30 miles away from my niece's house.) (Eye opener: Why did he go this far to take her some tea that she could have bought where she lived?) This did not make any sense at all. He obviously misread my intelligence. I am truly saved and able to tolerate more than the average woman. I may have appeared to be naïve at times, but I am no fool. Without a doubt, something was brewing between Denise and Barry, and it wasn't tea.)**

Now, it was approaching time for us to leave Denver, and as soon as we returned home, he did not waste any time getting started with his foolishness all over again. Now that I am aware that he is able to control his anger, I should have not have to accept anything less from him. Immediately, upon our arrival home, he went into the garage at about 2:00 a.m. in the morning to put up a FOR SALE sign. Soon after our arrival, we received a telephone call from Denise. I told him that I would call her later;

he was extremely irate with me. His excessive doggedness and desire for me to contact her right away made me very suspicious about the two of them. **(Awareness: Based upon his actions, I knew in my heart that they had taken their friendship to another level).** It was just a confirmation to me when this happened. Just before this occurred, I had given him a kiss in the hall, and instead of him embracing me back, he came into the room talking very loud to me about not responding to Denise's phone call. **I felt very weird about this episode because we had gotten along so well while we were in Denver. Now, we are on the war path once again. He is acting like a mad man all over again. I spent a ton of money for this trip; we stayed there for 30 days, and this is the thanks that I get.** I paid for the flight there and gave my niece a little stipend for her hospitality. In addition, I paid for our meals, and we used my nephew's car the entire time we were there. **(Awareness: He gets pleasant when he wants me to do something for him; then, he changes after it is done. It appears that Barry is a user from the bottom of his heart, and I am now truly realizing why he did not remain married to the previous wives. I am sure it was because of his behavior.)**

January 11, 2009 @ 2:29pm—Dear Journal, This is a day for me to meditate on all of my experiences during my visit to Denver. I am still in awe over the incident with Denise. She continues to communicate with Barry. I am so miserable.

He's a Fighter Not a Lover

(Chapter Seven)

February 4, 2009 @ 2:22 pm – Dear Journal, I am continuing to have marital problems. On January 27, I was too shocked when he asked me," When are you going to be ready to walk?" I replied, "Whenever you are ready to walk." He got angry and told me that I was mean to him. After this conversation, we did not speak to each other for about a week. It is obvious that he is finding any reason to get angry. It is my belief that it is because of his relationship with Denise. <u>I am sensing that he and Denise are talking secretly. I have reached this conclusion because one day, while we were in Sam's, she called his cell phone, but he walked off to talk to her. Another time she called, he said that she wanted to know what to do about a car problem. I told him that she had a brother and other friends there who could help her, but he said that she wanted his expertise.</u> **(Awareness: Both Barry and Denise disrespected me and did not care. From this moment on, I was aware that she was instigating their friendship.)** <u>To add fuel to the fire, he told me that we are headed for a divorce.</u> Frankly, I am getting tired of his lies and deception, so I really do not care anymore. This time, <u>he did not apologize to me so I have a huge suspicion that she is the perpetrator and is behind his slight change in behavior; this adds fuel to a fire that is already lit.</u> He was already crazy, but when she came along, he became worse. We are really estranged now, and I just go about my daily routine and ignore him. <u>I joined an exercise program this month, and now I am going to take care of me.</u> **(Awareness: It was not a wise idea for me to cater to Barry's needs and desires and allow him to control me. He disrespected, manipulated, used and abused me. Our marriage was already on a downhill dive, but Denise probably provided him with even more negative ideas in an effort to terminate our marriage and possibly take their friendship to another level so that she could have him for herself. I should have taken more interest in**

taking care of my own needs much earlier instead of paying more attention to his.)

March 13, 2009 Friday @ 6:00 pm –Dear Journal, <u>I am absolutely certain that my husband has a mental problem because right now we are going through it again, and I do not know why except he wants me to just leave.</u> He has been giving me the silent treatment and the cold shoulder since Wednesday. I cannot trust this relationship any longer. About two weeks ago, I was ill with a sinus infection so bad that I had to get into bed for a few days. He did fine for two days, but after that, he left me to fend for myself. <u>He left me and stayed away from home the entire day; he did not lift a finger to call me. I think that Denise was in town at that time. Another strange incident happened one day when he brought another woman into the house and said that she was his cousin. I was in bed sick, and they went into the living room talking. With my door closed, he played the piano for her while I was in the bed. He told me that he took her and her mom to get some food; then, he took her home. He stayed gone for two hours or more.</u> He is very much so out of line in doing this to me, but I know that payday is coming for him. When he left, he asked me if I would be okay. I told him "yes" because I was beginning to dislike him for treating me so cruel. My husband treats everyone better that he treats me, and I am the one who is always available for him. Several times, while we were out, he complimented other women on their appearance. <u>In fact, he told Denise that she was pretty and sexy right in front of me. He is so disrespectful and out of control</u>. I am not feeling this relationship at all, and I want to find a peaceful way out. He has already made it known to me that he wants out so it is just a matter of time. **(Awareness: <u>I have given him my all and all; so, I do not feel bad about breaking up at this point because I was better than a good wife to allow this man to disrespect me, strip me down of all of my money, and allow him to take a big bite out of my life</u>.)** I am not cheating on him, but I have found my peace without him by working out, losing weight, and seeking God Almighty for my high calling in Him. I don't know how much more of him that I can take; I am waiting on my breakthrough. The other day, he was sick when I left to go to exercise and to run some other errands. He called and asked me what I was doing. I told him that I was running errands for our family reunion. <u>He asked me to stop by the house to pick him up because he wanted to ride with me. I started not to do it, but I did because I just cannot be mean to people</u>. **(Awareness: <u>I needed to just leave him to alleviate this problem. Maybe, now I am the one with the problem. He has done so much wrong to me, and I am still nice to him.</u>)** After I picked him up, I went by my daughter-in-law's job to drop off some papers. **After that, I took him down town to Wild Wing's for lunch in City Market. (Awareness: I am just a big sucker for people, and I guess that is why they use**

me so badly.) I have been nice to people all of my life. It did not just start with Barry. Some of them took advantage of that nice spirit in me, but not to the extent that my husband has taken. **(Awareness: He is literally abusing our covenant as husband and wife. I have been awesomely supportive of him, but he is using me to the fullest**.) The Lord forbids his deception because Barry's day of reckoning will not be so good. God's word says not to touch or afflict His anointed ones.

April 10, 2009 –Dear Journal, It has been a while since I have visited. Today is Good Friday, a holiday. I have had a terrible year this far, but thank God I am balancing out now. Barry is back on the trail of Mr. Nice Guy again after another silent episode for no reason. Last week, Barry approached me with a warm hug and wanted me to embrace him back; I did with reservations. He keeps hell inside of his heart and shuts down. When he feels good or up to something, he is kind again and wants to become intimate with me. I know for a fact that he needs professional help, but he is bucking that. He could get some help from the *More Than Married* Seminar sponsored by our church, but he does not want to attend. Sometime ago, I bought a DVD entitled *Fireproof Your Marriage,* but he will not watch it. I pray to God that he will try to seek enrichment for our marriage; otherwise, our marriage is doomed. He is a good man, but MOST of the time, his spirit is STUBBORN; he is very mean, hateful and nasty. In spite of all that he has done and said to me, I am trusting God to heal Barry. I cannot help but remember how good my life was before entering into this marriage covenant with Barry. The only entity that was missing was a partner to share my life; then, he came along at a very vulnerable stage of my life. I don't know why, but I will continue to pray for changes to come into our marriage because I am not a quitter. It is so embarrassing to have waited so long to get married; then, allow someone like Barry to come into my life and ruin it. God is a God of change, and I look to HIM to CHANGE Barry. Sometimes, I get so confused, and then I go to my WORD to get strength to endure. Although I have grown weary in my well doing with Barry, lately, he has not been there to ease my pain. Instead, he has been on my case to pressure my tenant to purchase my rental property. I am not sure that this is what needs to happen at this point, but I have been talking to her about buying it. She explained that she is getting very close to qualifying and later purchasing my home. **(Awareness: I am discerning that Barry is also after this money to either blow on himself or on another trip; hence, I am being very cautious about this subject.)** Tonight, we are both participating on the Easter Program at the church; he is playing in the church band, and I am singing in the church choir. We have had lots of rehearsals, and we are both excited about the program tonight. Actually, we have had a few pleasant days and we are trying to enjoy each other's company for a change. I would love for us to stay like this. I ask you God "please give us the wisdom and understanding in our marriage and intercede by sending us help." Tyrese and Cherlyn, our son and his wife, are younger than we are, but they have been jewels in several counseling sessions with Barry and me. I know that they are growing because they interjected many words of wisdom in our discussions.

May 23, 2009 @ 10:58 am—Dear Journal, It has been a while since my last visit. Today is Saturday, and I am not feeling my best; I have had congestion. Barry was ill two and a half weeks ago. It seems as if the germs lingered in the house in spite of my cautious actions of spraying disinfectant, and I caught his cold. I am feeling better now, but I'm not "out of the woods" yet. Our relationship seems to be much more unified and is much better than usual. We have not had any major problems since March 13, 2009, which is about two months now. A great deal of our "peaceful time" is because we both have been sick. On May 20, I emailed him a sweet little note letting him know how much I appreciate his attentiveness towards me when I was ill, and I told him that I love him and wanted us to work on our relationship as diligently as possible. He never said a word to me about this email, so, I asked him about it, but he refused to say a word to me. He just does not know how to be lovable or maybe he just refuses to be kind. I know that he is able to show this kind of kindness towards me because he had a different demeanor when we dated in 2005. Every now and then, he releases himself to do pleasant things, but now it is very seldom. The other night, while we were watching the game, I asked him a simple question about the game. He responded by smart mouthing me with arrogant words. After that, he "blew up" with an attitude and stopped speaking to me again. I emailed him again to express how crazy I thought his actions were, and I went a little further and expressed that I really did not think that his actions were about what I had asked him. **(Awareness: At this time, it became necessary for me to tell him that I felt that it was about his upbringing and a number of other agitated areas of his life.)** In addition to him not being satisfied or happy with me any longer, he is saying that he does not care to mall walk with me any longer and that it is better for him to walk by himself. I said okay because he is not happy and wants to make me unhappy along with him. Now, he is bad mouthing me for everything that I do not deserve, but I continue to hold my peace. For example, he said, "If you don't want to be married to me, do what you have to do to get a divorce because I do not have a gun on you." He continued to say, "I made it before you, and I will make it after you are gone." I think all of this is just foolish crazy talk; **(Eye opener: This was wishful thinking.)** I am going to wait on the LORD to intercede for me. "Lord, you know my heart and my desire; therefore, I am looking to you for a permanent answer to this situation. Father, I waited for a very long time for a husband, and this is what I have gotten." **(Awareness: I know that it must be a purpose for me being in this man's life.**) Please show your face strong in this relationship. **I am not feeling comfortable at all with him these last days of my life; it is like a world wind blowing in and out. (Awareness: Save me from this _Nightmare on Ashford Street._ I thought after all these years and his previous marriages (I believe about 6 others). He would want to change for the better. Obviously, I was very wrong about my decision to marry him.) (Eye opener: I was unaware that Barry had been married twelve plus times.) Our anniversary is next Tuesday, June 2nd and it feels like Hell in this house. My heart hurts because I missed God big time when I married Barry Lovett. June 2nd means nothing to him or to me at this point**. I went to visit our pastor at the church the other day and explained my entire situation to him and I am hoping that he will talk to Barry and me about our marriage. Maybe he can explain to Barry better than I can what it means to be married. I have always told Barry that marriage spells WORK, but he has not comprehended this message.

June 10, 2009 on Wednesday night – Dear Journal, It was an awesome covenant fellowship and a fantastic day that I experienced on Wednesday. I attended Bible study; unfortunately, he missed it and came later for band practice. **(Awareness: I really wanted him to go with me to Bible study, but he must have a desire to attend it on his own.)**

June 11, 2009 on Thursday – Dear Journal, Our son, Tyrese and his family left to visit Carowinds Amusement Park with their church family. One of my other niece's came by to visit us with her cute little boy. Nikki stayed a while, and we took her son to another niece's house because I was about to treat him to a dinner date at a local restaurant that evening. We enjoyed our meal; afterwards, we went to Sam's so that I could buy some groceries for the house. **(Awareness: It's about time that I stop treating him to dinner and insist that he treats me sometimes.)** We both had some things to do; consequently, we went our separate ways until that evening.

June 12, 2009 on Friday – Dear Journal, On Friday, I picked up my best friend from the car repair shop and took her to work before I went to exercise. Shortly afterwards, I did a little shopping for Barry; I bought him a dress shirt today as a Father's Day gift. I have always had Barry's best interest at heart, but I am truly overjoyed that I am now taking an interest in myself. **(Eye opener: I should have taken an interest in myself earlier. Perhaps, Barry may have been more respectful towards me with words and actions. When we love ourselves, others realize it and respect us for it.)** I have lost ten pounds and 21 inches since I have started exercising on February 10, 2009. I am exceedingly proud of myself. Tomorrow, to celebrate Father's Day, we plan to attend church together followed by a delightful dinner for two at a Japanese restaurant.

June 13, 2009 8:45am—Dear Journal, This is a Saturday morning, and I am not happy. My husband and I have been on bad terms for two weeks due to a lot of foolishness. After talking to his sister in New York and Cheryln (our daughter in law), I decided to prepare a salmon dinner for him on Wednesday evening June 3. I called him to the table to eat, and he came. We had not spoken to each other from May 22 to June 3. I tried to talk to him, but he did not respond to me or my emails to him. He responded to one email because he found an opportunity to lash out at me in it. He capitalizes on any and everything that is negative. The email that he responded to was about his attitude and how it must have come from his upbringing. As stated before, he "blew me out". The pleasant email that I sent him was ignored because it was about love. **(Awareness: Our pastor articulated that based on what *I told him about Barry, he does not know how to love.* He also said that it sounded like Barry would rather fight than love, and he was exactly right. When I shared with Barry that I had gone to confer with the pastor, and asked if he would go to the counseling session with me, he stated that he did not need another man telling him what to do.)**

June 19, 2009 @ 7:05pm— Dear Journal, I am feeling much better but it feels like I have been through a world wind again. Last Sunday after church on June 14, Barry stated that he wanted out of the relationship once again. Pastor preached from Psalms 37, which is about evil doers. He stated that the steps of a good man are ordered by the Lord. You would think that it would have touched Barry in a positive way, but his mind shifted into his evil ways and he had gotten angry with me. During this time, my niece was staying with us because of a brief illness. He was very nice to her as he is with everyone he encounters. **(Awareness: He puts on a false face around others).** She was treated as royalty by both of us while she was with us, but there was a great deal of coldness in the air towards me. One morning at breakfast, my niece told Barry that she knew one of his former wives and told him that they were friends. He began to talk negatively about that wife to us. I just knew that he was lying on her based on my experience with him. **(Awareness: He is a great actor and pretender when he is involved in uncomfortable situations; most of the time, he pretends to like people when deep down in his heart he does not. You never know if he is truthful or deceitful because the minute your back turns, he is talking bad about folk.)** That morning at the breakfast table may have impacted his behavior with me after church because he knew that my niece had befriended one of his former wives.

She may have known something about their history together. Barry was adamant about spending the rest of his time alone that Sunday. (Awareness: He appears to be a schizophrenic because his personality changes into a werewolf, and it is very scary to me.)

June 21, 2009 on Sunday evening – Dear Journal, Barry apologized about his actions and behavior and asked me if we could start all over again. I accepted this once again, and we have been doing fine for one week now. **(Eye opener: It is possible that my niece's comment about his former wife forced him to face himself and the reality that our failing marriage was probably his fault.)**

June 29, 2009 early Monday morning –Dear Journal, We left home to visit Hilton Head, South Carolina where we enjoyed our first date after getting back together in June of 2005. We spent the day sightseeing. Later on, we visited the beach for a short while. Next, we shopped at Sam's wholesale and the Hilton Head shopping center where we dined at Fuddruckers for lunch. Once again, he informed me that he did not have any money, and, as always, I took care of the bill. **(Eye opener: In my opinion, Barry probably needed to "get away" and needed my resources to facilitate his whims. He is still an actor and a user. I don't trust him.)** Our jaunt at Hilton Head ended when it started raining hard all of a sudden. Not wanting to be caught in a thunderstorm, we finished eating lunch and returned home. By the time we had returned home, it had stopped raining which gave us an opportunity to walk in the mall. I am really trying not to talk to him a great deal, and I am treating him with "kid gloves" or in a softer voice tone for peace sake.

A Dead End to Real Issues

(Chapter Eight)

August 10, 2009 —**Hello Journal,** It has been a long time since my last visit. As a matter of fact, my entries into the computer while assisting Tyrese with coordinating the events for our family reunion have required a great deal of my time. Today is my birthday. I can vividly remember that after church on Barry's birthday, I treated him to fine dining at a Japanese restaurant; then, we went to purchase an MP3 player as a birthday gift to him. When we returned home that day, July 2009, we got into the Jacuzzi and had a pleasant evening without any contention. Today, I suggested that we set out to the Hilton restaurant because one of my girlfriends sent me coupons to use on the "two for one" special. He agreed, and we went there for lunch today. **(Awareness: Frankly, I feel that if I had not suggested celebrating my birthday and using the coupons, we would not have left the house to do anything**.) To back track a bit, the coordinator of our family reunion, my son Tyrese, planned an immensely enjoyable and memorable occasion, and all of the events were implemented to perfection. My sister stayed with us for two weeks and one of her daughters and her two children stayed with us for two nights during the family reunion. Barry put his chef's hat on and whipped up some delectable food for my sister and my niece and her children, but he was very selective about inviting other family members to dinner. As a matter of fact, he only invited the ones he said "he liked" over to our house for dinner. I must give him his rave review; he can cook well when he is in a good mood. On the other hand, if Barry is in a bad mood, he behaves irrationally. For the most, everything went well. During this time, my heart wanted me to believe that we had actually started all over again because we had been getting along very well until my sister left on Wednesday, August 5th. After my sister boarded the plane to Texas from the family reunion, immediately, Barry's attitude significantly changed once again.

While driving from the airport, Barry complained that I had prepared his coffee too strong that morning; he "came at me" as if I did it intentionally. Brigette, another granddaughter, was with us in the car as we returned from the airport. Even in her presence, he acted up very badly. She was able to get a glimpse of her granddaddy's bad attitude. She was really shocked to find out that he was so mean and hateful for no reason at all. He stopped talking to me for a few days and because Brigette was with me, she got the cold shoulder right along with me. She had spent two nights with me while her grand aunt was visiting with us.. **(Awareness: As stated before, the phony, fake, bogus "Mr. Nice Guy" Barry was too long suppressed. "Front or Sham Time" was over the minute my sister was on that plane headed to Texas. He seems to possess a Dr. Jekyll and Mr. Hyde personality—the duality of the good and evil in human nature. With me, however, his evil nature seemed to override his good. I am convinced that he has some serious mind problems. He just has to be angry about something, and he is also very negative about people and situations. He does not like many people, and he tries to keep my spirit low. I have asked God Almighty to touch and change his life, but so far it is not working on a permanent basis. His mind is like a yo yo—up and down. You never know how he is going to act on any given day. My husband is a mad man, and right now he is not satisfied with playing in the church band. He dislikes most of the band members because according to him, no one is doing what they are supposed to do except him. He separates himself from everyone and never socializes with anyone at the church. I guess he is hiding his TRUE self from them. He is probably afraid to spend too much time around them because they will eventually discover the REAL Barry. I am absolutely certain that he does not want that to happen.)**

Once again, Barry's unreasonable behavior surfaced due to a situation involving my oldest son, Maurice. One Sunday after church, Maurice and one of my sisters who lives in Savannah came over to the house. Barry became very upset about Maurice's visit because Barry detested Maurice to the point that he had already requested a restraining order to prevent him from coming to the house. Barry did not consider the fact that Maurice's daughter, who was residing with Barry and me just prior to our family reunion, needed to talk with her father who she had not seen since she was an infant. Instead, he became angry with my 12 year old granddaughter just two days before the reunion and, for spite, he sent her on the airplane back to Denver. **(Awareness: Only a mentally deranged individual would do such a cruel thing. I could not do a great deal about it because he seemed really crazy, and I was not sure what he would do to me if I had allowed her to stay against his will. I was aware of Barry's sickness; he was seemingly psychotic/neurotic at**

that time. Thanks to God for the things he has done within my family. Prior to my family's gathering, Barry predicted that we would have a disaster at the beach and that we would have some serious trouble with certain family members as well. None of those negative predictions happened because everyone followed the rules and was obedient to the plans. Everything went quite well to his surprise. **(Awareness: He was very hateful about the beautiful outcome of the entire agenda. I have never seen such a bad spirit because of unity within a family, but once again he comes from a totally different environment than my family.)** My family members can have disagreements and fall out for a brief moment, but then, we are all back to loving on each other again. **(Awareness: Barry does not understand that kind of behavior at all and was trying with all of his might to make me be like him, but I refuse to be like him.)** I really love my family and will always love them no matter what they do or say because I believe that God will eventually touch their hearts and we will prevail with prayer. He hates my sister and my oldest son. Sometimes, I think he hates his own granddaughter. He is always saying that she is too big and wears inappropriate clothing with big earrings. He says that she is ruined because her parents allowed her to have a cell phone too early. He wants her to remain a little girl and he and I get into it a LOT about Brigette. I feel that he should be praying about those things instead of talking her down to me and God knows who else he is talking to about her. He also talks about the other grand children saying that their mother may not know it, but he believes that the oldest girl has been sexually active and the other girl is overly developed and headed in the wrong direction. According to him, he hates his daughters, but he changes faces when they come around. **(Awareness: He is dangerous, and at this point, I do not trust him at all.) (Eye opener: Usually a person who is a complainer, an outsider, moody, right about everything, and hates his own children and grandchildren has some serious mental issues.)** Because of Barry's negative actions towards toward Brigette and me, I contacted Tyrese and explained how his dad was treating us. Without delay, he left his job to pick up Brigette to take her home. Before he picked her up, Tyrese called the house. After Tyrese's call, Barry began to talk more pleasantly to me. His entire personality changed when Tyrese came over to the house to get his daughter. **(Awareness: Barry continues to be an "academy award actor" by putting on fake and phony faces. Barry is a jerk for sure. At this point, I needed to get my PEACE back as soon as possible.)** The next morning, he asked me to go to the park with him. I consented to see what he was up to next. Now, we are talking again. The next morning, at church, the Holy Spirit inhabited the sanctuary so strong with the singing of anointed songs. Barry kept playing along with the church band members, but nothing significantly happened with him as it did with me and others in attendance. I was lost in the spirit for a few hours along with several others, including the preacher. It was a travailing service which was "one of a kind". God was truly with us, and he tarried for about two hours after service was over. This experience went right over his head. Later on, he said, "I did not know what all that was about, but I just kept playing because of the other musicians." **(Awareness: God Almighty was in our presence and he did not realize it AT ALL. This is so sad.)** Sometimes, I feel so sorry for him for being out of touch with the Almighty, but there is nothing I can do for him at this point but pray that he will one day feel God's glory. He is definitely a fleshy person; nobody but God himself can change him. **(Awareness: As far as I can see, he is not growing in Christ. If anything, he is going backward and I just do not want to be in this relationship any longer.)**

August 20, 2009 @ 1:50am Hello Journal, I had to visit today because things are looking very bleak. On the 18th, Barry's sister and her boyfriend came to visit us from New York. They arrived on Tuesday evening. Both of us were happy to see them. His sister is a loving person, and we get along very well. Her fiancé' is also very nice and friendly. When they arrived, we were not doing well because last week Wednesday night after Bible study, I went home excited and ready to share the message with Barry, but he yelled "Is religion all you want to talk about?" He snapped at me so hard I was terrified. He carried that anger in his heart the entire time they were visiting with us. Even though he acted like a fool, I cleaned the house and went shopping preparing for our visitors, his sister and her fiancé'. He is treating me wrong by acting as if I am nothing to him. I cannot take much more of this emotional abuse. I feel as if my chest is coming out of my body. God please get me to the place of happiness again. He is a mean, nasty, and grouchy old man. **(Awareness: He is not happy with himself and that makes it impossible for him to be happy with me or anybody else. I learned today from his sister that he hates my hair color and does not want me to go to curves to work out. He has issues stacked on top of one another. He really needs Jesus in a BIG way, but I do not want to say anything ever again to him about the LORD.)** "Lord, please help me to cope with this madness until it is time for my exit."

August 27, 2009 on Thursday @10:50pm –Dear Journal, I am so worn out with this man; he is miserable with himself, and he is working over-time to make me miserable also. **(Awareness: At this point, I was really ready to give up on this marriage because I knew that I had done all that I could do to make it work.)** I thought we had a decent day; we went to the dentist for our teeth cleaning and after that we went to Belks to take my recycle bag for a new Mac lipstick. While there, he priced a juicer that was on sale, but before we purchased it, we walked to Macy's to price theirs. We decided on purchasing the juicer from Belk's. Next, we went to Piccadilly restaurant in the mall for lunch. I thought we had had a civilized fellowship during lunch. After that, we went to Publix for some pineapples, but he remained in the truck. When I returned to the truck, he asked me if I had seen his cousin in the super market. I told him "no", but I saw a male friend of mine from the past. Then, he asked, "Did he speak to you?" I responded, "Yes." When we returned to the house, he was acting strange. I ironed some clothes from the laundry basket. Then, I asked Barry if he wanted me to juice him a drink. He said, "Yes." He left the house once again to pick up his prescription from the drug store while I juiced the drink. When he returned, he continued to act strange. I had a feeling that while he was away, he had been on the telephone with Denise, the niece through marriage that lives in Colorado. I continued to iron the laundry when he returned. I served him the drink and went back into the blue room to finish my chores. After my chores, I prepared a light snack, went to our bedroom, and watched some movies on the movie channel that Brigette had mentioned to me earlier. **As soon as I went into the room, he asked me if I thought we were going to make it. I paused for a while and then I asked him, "Do you think that we are going to make it? He responded, "I am tired of pretending and putting on a front for people; we do not have it anymore." I paused again for a longer period of time to think about what Barry had said. His response was so deep that I had to be careful about my response to him.** Then, I said, "If you don't love me, it must be miserable being with me; if you want a divorce, I will be okay with it. Don't worry; I will be alright because I know that God wants what's best for my mental health. I knew we were heading in this direction anyway. I know what belongs to me and what belongs to you in this house. I also told him that we did not have to fight about property. I told him that I want to be happy, and I have done all that I know how to do to make him happy, but it just did not work. You have so many rules about what I should or should not say and about who I should or should not speak to or to be around. Sometimes, you say I talk too much, and the list goes on and on. Sometimes, I don't know what to say, so I don't say anything. I need love and affection not someone jumping all over me and getting angry about everything under the sun. I waited a very long time to be married and this is what I have gotten." Then, I told Barry that Cherlyn saw his former wife today at her high school and that she touched her on the shoulder and said, "Hello". Cherlyn said that she appeared happy. He did not talk to me for a while for saying that. I asked him to do me a favor. Barry said, "What?" I said, "When we get the divorce, please let me know. Please do not surprise me like you did with the wife before me. I would like to be able to plan my exit so that I won't be in a mess." I did not get a response from him. **(Awareness: I really think he is crazy and will never be satisfied with anyone especially a wife. Last night, our preacher spoke from his heart about being spirit filled, and the mes-**

75

sage always goes over his head like "a flock of lame ducks". I just don't understand how God allowed me to miss HIM when I decided to marry Barry Lovett. I have decreed and declared his walk with the Lord so many times and now I just do not know what else to do. <u>I realize that he cannot love me because he does not love himself.</u> When I look at him, I see a miserable person. I see someone with a great deal of baggage who does not know how to unload the weight. He can't even understand that that weight is killing him softly. He fills his mind with negative thoughts and holds onto so much mess until he cannot see when someone right by his side is trying to open his eyes to the understanding of God's Truth which is the only thing that will set him free. He will not allow himself to be purged, healed, and delivered from the sins of this world. It is very sad to live that way, and I feel sorry for him because he is perishing and don't even know it. I am a person who loves people, and when I go to church to get fed the *Word* of God, I get revived again and again and that causes me to want to share and spread that joy with others. He goes to church to play his instrument, but he leaves immediately following the service to head for home. No one knows him on a personal level as they know me. When I discussed this with our pastor, he said that it sounds like Barry is treating our church service as a "gig" where he will go play his "gig" and then leave. I have decided that I will not fight for something that is not real so if or when he files for a divorce with the right terms, I will definitely go along with the plan. I will pray, "God, continue to use me to be instrumental, if I can be, until we divorce and maybe someday the Holy Spirit will saturate his heart with the *Word* so that he can live and not die and go to hell." Even when I am no longer with Barry, I will pray , "LORD, PLEASE HELP HIM for I know that after my many experiences with him, it is my belief that Barry is really SIN SICK and SEEMS TO NOT LOVE GOD as a righteous person should.)

September 7, 2009 on Monday morning at 6:00am, Labor Day Morning- Dear Journal, I woke up at 5:00 am this morning. I just could not sleep, so I read Creflo Dollar's book *Creating the Life You Want;* I also read my *Bible*. Then, I prayed. I am still unhappy with my marriage and nothing in particular has happened, but it feels so strange and uncomfortable being around him. Now, Barry has been sick since last weekend. To remedy his physical challenge, today, he went to see his doctor whose prognosis was that he had the "swine flu" and that he needed to be homebound until he recovered. <u>Even though Barry was stricken with the flu, he was adamant about playing the church band. My belief is that his playing in the band does not reflect his genuine dedication to God, but it is doing something for God to be seen on TV.</u> . **(Awareness: When we watch**

the church's television broadcast, his statements are "They never keep the camera on me. Sometimes, they don't even show me." This is vain glory.) Because of Barry's physical condition we did not attend church the following Sunday; instead, we stayed home, and I took care of him. (Awareness: I am still compassionate towards him even though I know he is a devil.) He pulled himself together and drove himself to the family cookout on the island park for about two hours. He wore gloves and a mask and took them off to eat some fish and potato salad. Then, he went home. I returned home about 6:00 pm. My family had a lot of fun at the cookout. We played dodge ball, cards, and listened to some first-rate music while we ate some scrumptious food. I took a few ribs and some chicken home, and this was our dinner. We watched television for a while; then, we took our meds. I had to take his medicine in order for me not to get the swine flu. We are sleeping in separate bedrooms for my protection. I am keeping all of the clothes clean, the environment clean, and doing all of the preparation of meals. Last week, I made some homemade chicken soup and shrimp Creole. He said that it was delicious and that he enjoyed it, but it seems as though he just does not like me no matter what I do for him. It seems as though the very sight of me irritates him. At breakfast, I told him that I know that he does not like or love me anymore. He denied it, but I know for a fact that he is lying about it. He has been quiet because he needed me to care for him through his sickness. (Awareness: A woman always knows if her husband loves and adores her. My husband is a user and a fighter; he is not a lover at all towards me. When my investment funds were depleted, he took his anger to another level.) The Holy Spirit has already told me that my husband has another agenda and it does not involve me. He treated me so badly when his sister and her fiancé' were visiting us, I was so embarrassed by his actions. He certainly is not happy with me anymore, and it is quite obvious. One evening, he made really rude comments to me concerning the computer, and he whispered nasty comments about our granddaughter. His comments were so offensive and abusive that I could not bear them anymore; I went into the bedroom and cried. Tyrese and Cherlyn came over here on Friday the 28th to talk to us about our marriage. They did a great job. After that session with Tyrese and Cherlyn, he pretended that he will try to do better, (Awareness: There is too much magic missing in our marriage now, and I am afraid that it is too late for us. We are never intimate with one another and that is a very important area in any marriage. His complaint to me is that I have said too many things to him to turn him off. Well, he is not alone. I am totally turned off by his nasty behavior and bad attitude. At this point, I do not even want to become intimate with him.) I would prefer to continue to sleep in another bedroom away from him than to sleep with him. I ask you God, "Please point me in the right direction because I know that I am married to a mad man. "

September 17, 2009, Thursday, Dear Journal, Today, we spent some time together. We went to get my back windshield wipers replaced. He said that he would take care of it for me, but he ended up asking me for the money because he said that he left his money at home by mistake. **(Eye opener: Actors, fakers, phonies always have excuses. He did not intend to pay for the wipers. Barry is all "talk and game". He is a deceitful and unhappy man.)** After my windshield wipers were replaced, we went mall walking. I was hoping that we would discuss what we will do with our marriage, but we didn't. Later, we went to Sweet Potatoes for dinner. He did not say very much to me there either, **(Awareness: He treated me because I told him go back home for his money; after all, I paid for the windshield wipers) (Eye opener: I was aware of Barry's lies and the deceitful games he had played in order to use my money and not use his. For this reason, I reminded him to get the necessary funds for dinner.)** After dinner, we went to Sam's and Wal-Mart so that I could buy some food for the house. We are getting along better but our marriage stinks. I stayed home for two days because last night I went to a *Breakthrough Conference* at the church and got home about 10:00 pm. Although I know that he does not love me, he is very negative about me being out late. He called and left me a negative message on my cell phone before I was out of church. He does not trust me, and I have never given him any reason to feel that way. **(Awareness: I suppose it is because he is not doing what he is supposed to do by me and that raises his suspicion about what I am doing other than serving God. It is strange that people, who do not do what they are supposed to do, worry about what others are doing.)** Before I go out with someone else and have a love affair, I will leave him first because I do not believe in cheating as he obviously does. On Sunday, when we came home from Barnes, I tried to embrace him but he rejected me by pushing me away. **(Awareness: I guess I am trying too hard to make something out of what is nothing but pure stupidity. I am not feeling him at all these days, but I just wanted to test him once again.)** It seems as though he is trapped with having a bad mind, and it feels almost as if he hates me for no reason. I believe he hates my walk with the Lord. Later on that day, I informed Barry that I would like to attend a free concert downtown, but he did not say a word to me about it. He kept his silence and proceeded with his day. Afterwards, he went to pick up some fried fish, shrimp, and some cold slaw and brought it home for dinner. We did not go to the concert because he wanted to watch football all day long on television, so I decided to stay in the blue room to watch movies today. My life is the pits; I can't even go to a free concert these days. I enjoy staying at home for the most part, but, from time to time, I enjoy going out to socialize with other people. All I ever do is go to Curves of which I love doing, but his sister informed me that he does not want me to even go there. In addition to Curves, I attend Bible study and choir rehearsal on Wednesday nights. Lately on Sunday mornings, we have been leaving together to attend church services; we practice at 9:40am on Sunday morning; then, we go into the sanctuary at 10:30am for the worship service.

Every Sunday, we are at home about 1:00-1:30 pm. unless I suggested that we go out to eat. <u>Of course, he insists that I pay the bill when we go out.</u> Sometimes, he would cook something for Sunday dinner on Saturday night before going to choir rehearsal. I love participating in my church activities. I also enjoy my home life, but I would rather have a balanced life as well. This is a critical stage in our lives. <u>Usually, when we get home from church on Sundays, we stay there for the rest of the evening with no excitement of any kind. We are just in the house together without any excitement going on if you know what I mean.</u> I pray, "Lord, I ask you for the 100th time what should I do? <u>I don't feel like an old and run down person. I feel that I have a great deal of life left inside of me, but he is sooooooo dead. All he wants to do is cook and eat, and if we go somewhere, it is just riding down River Street or downtown perusing the sites. He also likes visiting the old rundown neighborhoods where he used to live. He is extremely stuck in his past with excess baggage, and he just doesn't seem to have a desire to go forward. We do not have any friends to fellowship with because he does not like anyone. God PLEASSSSSSE change my situation where I can have my life back once again."</u> **One evening, I decided to send Barry a thank you ecard and another ecard for a small deed that he had done for me; he has not mentioned these gestures to me as of this date.** (Awareness: He is a mean and hateful man. My guess is that he is very miserable with himself. I think he can do better but the devil holds him back in bondage and he does not know how to fight for REAL life to enter into his life.)

September 19, 2009 on Saturday @ 11:50pm Dear Journal, The past week was very stressful to me. Barry and I are living under the same roof, yet I feel like a stranger to "my husband"; he's more like a "roommate". I have continued to serve him hands and feet as always, but he does not appear to appreciate it. After church on Sunday, I suggested that we go to Barnes restaurant to eat; he agreed, but he was not acting very happy with me these days. <u>His daughter called last night, and I answered the telephone. She was very rude towards me. I told him, "I am getting a restraining order if she does that again." He said, "Okay." Barry appeared very angry with me. He usually carries anger in his heart for days. My reason for saying this is because his angry expressions towards me are similar to those perpetrated towards my son, Maurice. I believe he has</u>

been talking about me to his daughters, but he refuses to admit his actions to me. **(Awareness: At any rate, we just don't have it anymore, and I really need to move on with my life.)**

Eye Openers:

- **Take notice when a man enjoys chaos**. That simply means that he would rather fight than love. In Barry's case, he was negative towards people and relationships. Beware if a man tries to kill your positive energy towards family and friends. Never let anyone keep you away from your family. Especially, take notice if he dislikes his own mother and family.
- **If a man disrespects you around others, he is showing off and looking for his own glory**. Barry argued about very small issues. This signifies that he had built up rage inside of himself that he needed to release at least once a week. I believe that Barry's rage was actually his demons of pride, envy, low self esteem, manhood insecurities, unforgiveness, deceitfulness, manipulation, adultery, and lust etc. inside of him that furiously wanted to surface with the ultimate intention of disturbing my peace.
- **In an effort to use my funds and assets, Barry manipulated me with mind games.** He would complain to me about people and look for sympathy from me as his reward. He thought up excuses or planned trips relying on my kind nature to withdraw funds from my retirement account or use my credit cards. He would indicate that these trips were a "feel good tool" to help him cope with life. Please be aware of this type of behavior. He is a schemer and all of it is deception, "a sham", or "an act". Be aware. "It is what it is". We women must face the facts.
- **Barry was also two-faced.** He would act one way in peoples' face, but behind their backs, he bashed them badly. He did this same thing to me. Be aware of back stabbers; he did this to his own sister that he claimed to have loved so much as well as members of my family.

Barry is miserable, and he seems to have worked "over time" to make me miserable as well. Do not allow anyone to steal your JOY and PEACE.

Selfish Desires

(Chapter Nine)

Saturday, September 26, 2009 – Dear Journal, <u>I went to a woman's conference; afterwards, I came home and decided to pursue him just to test his sexual ability, and it worked; he reciprocated. It did not last very long, but at least we were intimate after not having any activity for several months.</u> **(Awareness: I have been thinking that he could not have a sex drive because of his back pain, but that is so untrue. He is always angry, mad or just plain old ugly about everything is why he is distancing himself from me.** <u>When I counseled with the pastor, he asked me if Barry would rather fight than love. I can truly say that is a true statement about Barry.</u> **(Awareness: The** *Word* **of God states that the husband should love, honor, and cherish his wife, and I know that I am being cheated out of this truth because he seems to love, honor, and cherish his sister who lives out of town and a few other ladies in the church that he talks about and assist them up the stairs at church. This bothers me a great deal because I am the one that is here for him when he is sick and gives him financial support with everything that we do.)** As a matter of fact, I am the sole financier in this house. He pays the mortgage and his bills, but I pay everything else including groceries. **(Awareness: Now, I feel so abused and violated. The only thing that can get him on track is the** *Word* **of God, and he hates to talk about God, listen to God or pray that the** *Word* **of God would manifest in his life. Anyway, he holds a great deal of old baggage, and because of this, he cannot move forward.)**

Monday, September 28, 2009 of this week—Dear Journal, We went out and had a great day together. We also had a most delicious breakfast at Perkins. Then, we walked, shopped for groceries and other items at Wal-Mart. Later, we shopped at a seafood market for some crab meat; then, we returned home. I was in a cooking mood and prepared some crab cakes;

he joined me in the kitchen and whipped up some shrimp fried rice. The food was very tasty. We even had a pleasant afternoon for a change.

Tuesday night, September 29, 2009—Dear Journal, Barry went to band practice. Tyrese sent out a text message about what the family will do for the Thanksgiving holiday. Barry had a fit because he had already told me that he wanted a quiet day without any extras at the dinner table. He stated to me months ago that he wanted a low keyed holiday as he does most times when the holidays come around. Sometimes, he is okay with our son and his family coming over for dinner, but that is the extent of it. When he does invite someone over, it is to show off his cooking stills or brag about his personal possessions or seemingly accomplishments such as his garden, and his computer knowledge which our son taught him. **(Awareness: He brags about how comfortable he is at this juncture of his life, but the truth is that he is comfortable because I have invested my all and all into this relationship meaning time and money).** I tried to bring a fresh spirit into his life of which he liked my lifestyle as far as decorating the house and spending my money to make things comfortable, but he was not totally satisfied because he just cannot be happy too long with one woman. **(Eye opener: Barry cannot be happy because he does not have peace and joy within; instead, he has a void in his life. If he fills his spirit with daily Bible study, prayer to God, regular church attendance, and Christian fellowship, these things are able to produce the fruit of the spirit such as love, joy, peace , longsuffering, kindness, goodness, faithfulness, gentleness, and self-control (Gal. 5:22-23) etc.** He works overtime to try to make me dislike my family members, but I will always love my family no matter what he says. Because I am a serious-minded Christian, I can forgive people; whereas, he holds grudges for long periods of time and cut people off on a permanent basis if they make him angry. I refuse to be like him. God is a forgiving God, and he has forgiven me so many times for all of my sins and unrighteousness; therefore, I must do the same thing by other people. We do not have any friends because he does not like too many people. I want to socialize with the people at the church but he is always hurrying out the church to go home. As I stated before, he does not know many people in the church except for the choir members and the camera crew. **(Awareness: He is such a stand offish kind of person, and I am very different from him. I love people, and I love to fellowship with others. This makes us quite the opposite from each other.)**

It didn't take long for Barry to contact me about the text message from Tyrese; he was very negative about the Thanksgiving dinner arrangements, but I said nothing to him about it. When he had come home from band practice that night, we talked about his practice. Then, we ate dinner; however, I had to be very selective about what I would eat because it was the tenth and last day of my Daniel's fast, which is noted for God to reveal or uncover the mysteries in our lives. Not long after dinner, Barry took a shower and came into the family room where I was reading a book. He asked me whether I was upset about his feelings towards the preparations for Thanksgiving dinner. I responded, "no" but, I was concerned about an email that Denise had sent him." I proceeded to tell Barry. "When I sat at the computer to check my emails, I discovered that you did not sign out of your email. Then, I saw Denise's email message to you stating that she loved and missed you." He became very angry, loud, and extremely upset with me. He was in a rage and told me, "I am a grown man and no one will tell me who to talk to." His comment forced me to remind him about an assumedly inappropriate email that was sent by my sister's husband; he personally dictated my response back to him. My brother- in -law apologized to both of us and never sent out another email like that one again. My husband, if I can call him that, became fighting mad with me and told me that "he was sick of me and wanted me to get out of his life." He has not spoken to me since Tuesday night. When I came out of the shower, he had our bedroom door closed; therefore, I started sleeping in the blue room again. This was my confirmation that there is definitely an intimate relationship between Denise and him. All of the symptoms are there. He is doing extra mean things to me because of Denise.)

October 3, 2009 on a Saturday @ 3:00 pm. Dear Journal, A great deal more has happened since my last visit. It is so sad to say that Barry is not getting any better in his spirit. He holds so much garbage inside of his spirit until it is pathetic. Our pastor has been preaching out of the city of his soul, but Barry is not getting it at ALL. It seems to go right over his head. After leaving worship service, I have made comments such as "The anointing was flowing within the music ministry today". After observing other musicians and congregants who were under a heavy anointing —worshipping and lifting up holy hands, he would say, "I continue to play; I wonder what all that was about". I may have mentioned this before, but he will not go to Bible study unless he is playing. Because the choir director knows that Barry won't attend Bible study unless he is providing music, he asked Barry to play for Bible study so that he would attend it regularly. I recall asking him several times if he understood the message, but his response was "My mind wonders off elsewhere." **(Awareness: WOW what a waste! This man sits under a rich *Word* and won't receive what God's Word says. That is exactly what is wrong with him; he feeds his spirit with so much mess and cannot tap into the goodness of God. He gets up in the morning to "Archer Bunker", "Good Times", "Sanford and Son", and "The Jefferson's" which are all good, but he is living out some of these programs in his own life. When someone has a broken spirit, they should try to enrich their spirit with the *Word* of God, but**

not him. He won't pray or do anything that will help him to grow into the grace of God.)

October 6, 2009, Tuesday—Dear Journal, Lately, <u>he has done a series of terrible things to me such as turning off the air conditioner when it is hot, and now that it is cold, he turns off the heat.</u> He also has disabled the garage door, hid the notebook computer, tampered with the televisions so that they won't work, slammed doors in the house, threw out my sister's professional CD's of which she worked so hard on, took the cross off of the front door post, closed the Bibles in the house, made coffee just for himself, and most of all walked around like a mad man without a heart inside of his body. **(Eye opener: Barry knew that I had discovered his secret affair with Denise; therefore, he was doing everything in his power to cause me to become upset, irrational, and unhappy so that I would leave him. I decided to remain in the house to alleviate any charges of abandonment. Barry was really putting an all out effort in ridding himself of me.)**

October 10, 2009 on Saturday @ 11:36 am Dear Journal, I am still living in turmoil. Mr. Mad Man has been on the war path again since October 6, 2009 which was four days ago. I am anxious to see how long he will continue to behave in this manner.

October 11, 2009 on Sunday morning before church—Dear Journal, On several occasions, Barry appeared to be upset with me whenever I made journal entries. He probably felt that it would be a threat to him someday. For this reason, I could sense that he wanted to get rid of it. Even though I had hid my journal from him, when I left the house, he searched my room and found it.

When I arrived home from church, I asked him for my journal, and of course once again he denied it. I informed him that I knew that he had moved it because I know where I had placed it. <u>When I confronted him about it, he denied taking it, but said "I am not going to allow you to use your journal against me in court".</u> I told Tyrese about it, so Tyrese contacted him and asked him to return it to me. He denied that he had it, but I knew for a fact that it was in his possession because I had placed it under my mattress the day before. I ended up calling the police. The police stated that everything in the house was community property and it was nothing that he could do about it. Then, Barry called Tyrese on the phone crying and telling him that he did not do it. He also told him that he wanted his handicap card back for me first. Right then, I returned his handicap card. This issue was resolved when the children came over that evening to discuss our divorce. After they left and as I was preparing to go to bed that night, I found my journal in my dresser drawer. <u>I believe that Barry</u>

placed my journal into the dresser drawer while I was outside saying good night to the children. **(Awareness: Barry continues to lie and deceive.)**

October 18, 2009 on Sunday—Dear Journal, I did not sing at church today because Barry played with the church band, and I know that he is a devil. I just did not want to be up there in the choir stand with him. I mentioned the journal incident to the pastor and he asked me make an appointment to talk with him. Mr. Lovett is so nasty and ugly in all of his ways. I cannot understand why someone would bite the hand that feeds them. I have denied myself so much happiness by staying put in a "hell of a" marriage and not having the guts to get out once I knew who he was. I know that I am not God and would never try to be, but I honored God through honoring my husband even when I did not really want to. He has always been difficult to live with, but I tried with all of my heart to endure the pressure in hopes and having faith that he would change; instead, it got worse. I feel that I have given 110% of myself and have served him with every fiber of my being, but he still turned on me. Tyrese talked to us that Sunday evening and asked us a lot of questions. Then, when Barry discussed his mother, Naomi, he broke down crying like a baby and told Tyrese that his mom slept with different men in and out of the church; she even slept with the pastor of the church. He said that he thought that the men were hurting his mother because she was making loud noises, but it was all sexual activity. He said that he saw his mom do it over and over again. He was very disturbed about that situation. **(Awareness: I believe that his mom's actions were the main reasons for Barry being so screwed up mentally with women no matter how nice and respectful they are to him.)**

Over the years, Barry has distanced himself from his mother. He does not speak to her, and he dislikes almost everyone who comes too close to his "space". He has always tried to pull me down on his level of hate, but I refuse to do it. I pray for his mind to become transformed. When Tyrese spoke to his dad about life and encouraged him with words of wisdom, he refused to listen to good counsel. **(Awareness: He is a very stubborn man. I know that I must move on with my life at this point.)** Tyrese asked him if he would marry again because he firmly stated that we will not make it, and he stated that he will get a dog. Three has passed, since he last spoke to me. He went to an attorney for counsel and brought divorce papers home for me to sign. I told him that if the terms were right, I would sign. Then, he acted nasty and told me that I was a bitch and started calling me other names. **(Eye opener: Barry wanted the divorce on his terms; however, when he discovered that I was not about to be manipulated any more, he became angry and called me names.)** I found out through life experiences that "Everything is nothing if everything is all there is." Apart from GOD there is no point for life.

October 20, 2009 @ 9:00 am Tuesday morning—Dear Journal, as I sit here at my optometrist's office waiting to be seen, I am reflecting upon all the stuff that I have endured during my marriage. There have been so many traumatic things that have happened to me since Barry's been in my life. Now, I needed some legal counsel to help me get out of this tangled web of a dysfunctional marriage. In an effort to get a referral for a well qualified attorney, my girlfriend suggested that I contact my judge friend who was my colleague years ago at legal services. Not long after, I followed through and contacted my friend, and he gave me one of the top female attorneys in town. That same day, I contacted and explained to her that Barry was slamming doors and turning off the heating unit. She suggested that I purchase a heater and put on some ear muffs. After I told her that we did not have any small children and that we had been married for three years, she told me to call her back when I had been served the divorce papers. I followed her suggestion and bought a heater from Targets that same day. I tried desperately to cope with the situation at hand, but to add insult to injury, <u>Barry not only irritated me by the turning the thermostat up and down, he also took the garage opener from me, stole my cell phone, hid things from me, unplugged all the televisions, unplugged the washer and dryer, and the list goes on.</u> I started moving some of my things into storage because I can not continue on this journey that seems to never get to a peaceable end. I did not know when I would get out of this trap, but I knew I needed to somehow get out of it as soon as possible. <u>My niece and I packed boxes of books, some pictures, and other wall fixtures, and we placed them into storage at the end of October. At the beginning of November, we continued to pack some of the small items that belonged to me coming into the marriage. From September to October, I stayed gone most of the days and came back when it was time to go to bed to avoid any conflict with Barry.</u> **(Awareness: He wanted me out of his life so badly to the point that he did everything humanly possible to get me to leave, but I was waiting on a decent divorce proposal and the judge's final decision.)** In hindsight, when I married and moved in with him, I had a small yard sale to sell some of my kitchen and some other items. <u>Then, he forced me to give away all of my other furniture.</u> **(Awareness: Barry seems to be thinking if I leave him, he would be able to keep my bedroom suites that I brought into the marriage, but I am smarter than that. Also, he knows that he convinced me to give away my other furniture; he does not care about anyone but himself. He is sooooo selfish to have done this to me; yet, he continues to take, take, and take from me. I know that there has to be a reason for all of my suffering. One thing is certain; through it all, God has kept me.)**

November 23, 2009, Thanksgiving holidays, Dear Journal——. During the holidays, Barry invited his daughters and their families to come over for Thanksgiving dinner. This information was disclosed through my son when he contacted his sister to discuss their dad's and my relationship. I left the kitchen in good order with the glasses and china in the cabinet when they came. I just do not have a mean spirit inside of me, so I tried to work with him even though he is horrible towards me. He invited eight other people to live in the house with us while we are going through marital challenges. I knew that they were coming for Thanksgiving, but I was not aware that they were invited to live in the house with us. NOW THIS was a BIG surprise to me because they have visited our city on several occasions, but they never once lodged in our house with us. I had often times suggested that he invite them to stay with us before, but he would always tell me that they are nasty and unorganized people just like their mother and that he did not want them in our home. **(Awareness: I realize that the very reason why he invited them to stay at the house while I was still here was to aggravate me and force me to leave but I stuck it out even though they were pretty messy**.) The living arrangements were that he and one of his daughters slept on air mattresses in the family room and the five children slept on my king size bed in the master bedroom. His six year old grandson wet my bed. The third bedroom suite, which was my antique bedroom suite that I brought into the marriage, was occupied by the children's parents. **(Eye opener: He was really trying to break me, but I am strong in the Lord and the power of His might** He is quite aware that I like my home in a decent and respectable order. He even stated that the grand children did not know how to sit on the couch properly. The two older grands spent two nights with us last Thanksgiving and one of the girls removed and used the bathroom towels used for decoration to dry off her body. He said that they did not have any home training and that both of their parents have cheated on each other. He also told me that the older girls are now active and that their mother needed to be at home with them more. He talks bad about everyone even his own blood; it does not matter **(Eye opener: Anyone with any kind of wisdom and understanding should be able to discern, decipher, deduce, and deduct that if Barry gossiped about his own daughters and granddaughters, without a doubt he would have no reservations discussing someone else's flaws. Barry's actions are real examples of his backstabbing, lying, and deceitful personality flaws.).)** After Thanksgiving was over, his children left our fair city to return to their respective residences.

No More Tears; It Is Finished

(Chapter Ten)

On Sunday, December 6, 2009, Dear Journal—Because I had begun to have back pain, I asked Barry to sleep in his bed in the blue room where I had been sleeping, and I suggested that I sleep in my bed which was in the master bedroom; I had brought this bed into our marriage. When I made this request, he said, "Hell no! I am not giving up my room". **(Awareness: Barry became even more irate with me and began moving my bedroom suite into the garage. I had had enough of his games; therefore, after attending church, I stayed away from the house all day and returned that night.)** When I entered the house, I discovered that he had placed my bedroom suite into the garage and moved his bedroom suite into the master bedroom. My only recourse was to sleep on the antique bedroom suite, but he did not want me to sleep on the antique bedroom suite either, so he just moved everything around and had a mess going on in the house when I came home that night.

On December 7, 2009, about 10:00am —Dear Journal, I decided to ask him questions about locking my possessions in the storage shed; he became very angry and called me a "b" and a "w". Next, he said, "All I want you to do is to get the "F" out of my life." Then, he struck me as hard as he could with a closed fist, went into his room, and shut the door. **(Eye opener: Barry had mentally, verbally, and physically abused me. He knew that he was in deep trouble; that's why he closed the door.)** After Barry struck me, I left the house, and went to a neighbor's house to contact the police. I remained there until they arrived at the house. One of my nephews called me while I was at my neighbor's house. I explained the incident to him, and within minutes, he came over to see about me. I asked my neighbor to call our son that morning, but she was unable to contact him on the phone. Finally, the police and the ambulance arrived on the scene about the same time. The paramedics took my vital signs.

Because of the attack, my vitals were quite elevated. It was obvious that I needed further medical evaluation, and for this reason, they asked me if I wanted to go to the shelter or the hospital. My preference was to be evaluated by my private physician even though I was hurting very badly. After they left, my nephew drove me to my doctor's office. When I arrived at the doctor's office, I discovered that she was on vacation. My drive to the doctor's office was not in vain because her nurse took my vital signs and checked the bruised area on my chest. After that, she scheduled me to see another doctor at another location. **While traveling to the doctor's office, I called and spoke with my attorney and explained the details of this incident. She requested that I needed to report to her office the next morning.**

At the doctor's office, I had to endure several chest x-rays. After examining these x-rays, the doctor advised me to report to the emergency room in an ambulance because my heart was bleeding. Her prognosis was a "contusion of the heart". I started crying because I was terrified that I was going to die. My sister called me, and I told her about the doctor's report. She proceeded to console me with the love of Jesus Christ and that made me feel so much better. **(Eye opener: She contacted me at my weakest point. God knows when we need encouragement, so He worked through my sister to support me at the right time.)** She came to pick me up from the doctor's office that evening and took me to the hospital emergency room. Tyrese came to the hospital about 7:00 that evening. He called in another officer to view the bruise that had incurred from Barry's blow to my chest. By then, the bruise had turned purplish-red and had grown very large over my chest wall. Tyrese was quietly upset and furious about what had happened to me, so my sister and I asked him to cool off and leave. Later on, we told Tyrese and Cherlyn to retrieve my vehicle from the doctor's office and drive it to their home. My sister stayed with me at the hospital until about midnight. At that time, I was released with an understanding that I needed to receive follow up with my doctor in a few days. After leaving the hospital, we picked up my prescription for pain and proceeded to my son's home. The next morning, my sister arrived at Tyrese's home so that I could make my appointment at the attorney's office. My attorney filed a restraining order on Barry. I had to give myself some time to heal because I was hurting both physically and mentally from all of the attacks that Barry had committed upon me. During this time, God had to have been looking down upon me. "I thank God that I was able to reside with my son and his family during the Christmas holiday season." God always opens doors. I was so happy that I would not be alone. Instead, I could now enjoy a peaceful and loving family atmosphere during the holidays. I made every effort to start moving my personal belongings before the attack, but because of the injury that I had incurred along with the holidays, I had to put the moving on "hold" for a few weeks even though he had been restrained from the marital property. The pain in my chest was quite excruciating, and the bruise on my chest lasted for over six weeks. At least once a week as my health improved, my niece would come over to the house and assist me in packing my possessions. **ONE DAY, during the holiday season, the Holy Spirit spoke to me with a LOUD VOICE and instructed me to get both a marital and divorce background check on Barry. I did not think about it twice. I just obeyed the voice and decided to go to the courthouse to investigate his history of marriages and divorces. Once I arrived at the courthouse, I saw a friend of the family who is employed as the Lead Clerk of Superior Court in our area. She invited me into her office. After I told her what was going on with me and what I needed, she immediately began to research the system and we discovered that Barry had been married twelve (12+) times . All of his records did not show up in this county because he was smart enough to go elsewhere to get a marriage license, and of course, he played the system. (Awareness: I knew that he definitely had a problem, but I did not know that it was this severe. Thank God for the Holy Spirit leading me to retrieve this information. I was blown away by this news and just hoped and prayed that people will become more insightful about relationships and do their investigating before deciding to marry someone.)** I am so disappointed by all of his deception and lies. He was such a charmer when he came back into my life. I fell for all of his lies, and I mean he poured it on very strong until he conquered my heart once again. Then, I married him. As I stated before, he even went so far as making me believe he was speaking in tongues. As I think back on everything that was said and done, I realize that he must have been trying to kill me either mentally by trying to cause me to stay in a depressed state of mind or physically when he struck me in the chest over my heart and caused it to bleed. **(Awareness: I am now thinking back to the beginning of 2009 when he asked me if I had changed my life insurance policy to name him as my beneficiary on a policy with a large face value. I possessed this policy many years before he came back into my life. Even though I was reluctant in doing this, he pressured me into changing our son from the beneficiary and wanted me to name him as the irrevocable beneficiary on the policy, so I did it like a fool. It was coercion because I had reservations about doing it. On the day that I finally did it, I felt something deep down in my spirit telling me not to do it, but I wanted to please him so I did it anyway. It was only a few months later that we were in the state of finally breaking up, so I asked him to sign the form so that I could change it back to our son, but he refused to sign it; that confirmed my thoughts about him. I asked him, "Why would you want to be the beneficiary on my policy when we were breaking up?" Barry did not respond to me.)** No one on this side of the earth should be as gullible as I was with Barry. It is my sincere hope that I am doing some of you a great favor by sharing my story with you. **(Awareness: How was the insurance policy issue resolved? I decided to write the insurance company to explain my situation to them. I told them that he and I were getting a divorce and that he had attacked me to the point of my having a contusion of the heart. I also told them that he had refused to sign the form because he probably has plans to get rid of me and reap the benefits of the policy. I sent them a copy of the restraining order to show proof that he was indeed in trouble with the law; therefore, the insurance company agreed to change the insurance policy beneficiary's name from Barry's back to Tyrese.)**

On January 9, 2010, Dear Journal— We went to the Magistrate Court to prove his guilt in attacking me. My attorney represented me well that evening. We stayed in court until 6:00pm that evening, but we did not mind it at all because it was well worth our time and energy. The judge ordered that Barry be arrested for his violent acts towards me. He was handcuffed and ushered off to jail. I was finally getting some justice for the cruel and despicable actions perpetrated upon me. **(Awareness: As I reflect upon our years as a married couple, our marriage was basically lopsided— me giving and Barry receiving. It is utter disbelief that the husband that I invested my money, time, patience, and most of all my LOVE into would be so very cruel to me. He literally abused me mentally by calling me horrible names like "b" (rhymes with ditch), "w" (rhymes with door), and saying nasty things to me such as "I am sick of you" "Get out of my life." He abused me emotionally by being sparingly intimate and telling me that I was not good looking and pretty, and that I was not a Christian. He abused me spiritually by closing the *Bibles,* taking the cross off of the door, and most of all disallowing me to reverence God to the fullest. Yet, he presented himself as an "angel of light" when, in fact, he was a "demon in darkness". For example, he attended church to play in the church band, but his heart was empty and deceitful.** His behavior was so unpredictable and rude that it was obvious that Barry needed some help. I tried to get him some help by arranging two counseling sessions in May and again in October of 2009 with our pastor, but he refused. Because I was present at both sessions without Barry, these sessions really did not resolve our differences. In contrast, Barry made no attempts to seek counseling to help us improve our relationship. To make matters worse, neither our pastor nor his support staff took the initiative or time to help us reconcile our differences. To my surprise, Barry was even allowed to continue to play in the church's band without receiving any counseling. **(Awareness: Because I am a dedicated tither and had been a committed member of this church for six**

years, the church's lack of intervention and support during this time, forced me to take a very dim view of the pastor, and the band directors.) Barry joined this church in 2006 and started playing in the church band when I told my pastor that he was a musician. He played the organ and the bass keytah with the church band. Barry said that it was his way of tithing because that was what he did at his former church before he joined this church. He was very stingy about giving money to the church, so this was his way of getting out of tithing. When I gave money to the church, he made such a great scene about it as if I were doing something wrong. He has a distorted view about giving money to the church. I have decided to leave that church now so that I could find some peace concerning my marriage separation and my entire life events. I knew for a fact that my marriage was over in October 2009, but I stayed in it hoping and believing and praying for the Lord to do a perfect work in our lives. With all the baggage from his childhood and his multiple marriages, it is easy to say that Barry already had a lot of issues going on in his head; yet, he allowed Denise to manipulate and encourage him into her bosom. He was making plans for her to come be with him at our marital residence. I became aware of their plans when I overheard him saying, "I have a real nice set up at the house and you will be comfortable here." Then, he tried even harder to get me out of the house so that she could live with him. **(Eye opener: The man I married is so vindictive and abusive. I wonder how he could live with himself pretending to be someone that he is not. He tries to make people believe that he is so kind and loving, but believe me— there is always a motive behind that act. When he struck me, it was because he could not force me to leave the house otherwise. He "lost it on me" because I stayed in the house in spite of his foolishness and that made him angrier; especially, when I decided to question him about his cruel actions towards me.)** I was not supposed to say anything to him about what he was doing to me. All he wanted me to do was whatever he would tell me to do and to keep my mouth shut.

Even after he was ordered to be restrained from the property, on December 8, 2009, whatever his reason, he went back into the marital property on December 9, 2009. While he was there, he gave the cable boxes to their representative who had come to pick them up. I called Cable Company, and they verified the fact that he gave the boxes to their field representative. **(Awareness: This was another sign of his unruly nonconforming behavior that reveals a rebellious and disobedient spirit. He does not obey court orders or anything else if you ask me.)**

The next hearing was scheduled to be in the Superior Court on January 8, 2010, but the judge did not hear our case that day and continued it until February 5, 2010. Two of his daughters traveled long distances to support him in court. **(Awareness: This was very strange to me that Barry's daughters attended court because on several occasions, he used to** talk about them to me awfully bad. As I stated earlier, he acted as if he did not care for them at all; he just pretended and gave them a false impression when he spoke with them over the phone. He was just using them to aggravate me when he invited them to stay at the house for Thanksgiving, but I was gracious and kind to them in spite of his ploy.) It is also interesting to note that Barry's sister was there in the courtroom to support him as well. **(Awareness: He hated his sister who lives in town and on many occasions talked about her terribly bad as well; however, when he needed a place lay his head after being restrained from the marital property, he went to reside with her. This man will use anybody and anything as long as he can have his way in this world).**

I am writing this book to save people from destruction from people like Barry. He would smile in your face and stab you in your back when you are not looking. Back in the day, the Temptations had a hit song entitled, "SMILING FACES TELL LIES". The O'Jays also had hit tune "BACKSTABBERS". Barry epitomizes both of these songs in his dealings with people, especially, his MANY WIVES, FAMILY MEMBERS, and ME. Surprisingly enough, he even talked about the sister that lived away from here; I was too out done when he told her finance' that he was a Rolls Royce and not a Volkswagen; then, behind his back he said that his sister was using her for love and money. **(Awareness: He hated his sister's mother and stated that her mother took his dad away from his mother. He would never tell the truth about anything. In fact, he lies to people and make them think that they are on the up and up, but behind closed doors, he talks bad about them ALL.)**

Before the February 5th court date, the attorneys wanted me to get in touch with as many wives as possible to try to get their affidavits. I spoke with a few of them, but only one of them wrote an affidavit for the court.

- Once I contacted **wife number ten**, we agreed to meet for lunch. It was refreshing to know that she was very willing to write an affidavit to disclose the similarities in Barry's actions towards her and me. **(Awareness: She said that he charmed her into marrying him and stated that he would take care of her and her son very well, but after they moved into his house, he broke all of his promises. She stated that he is a great actor and lies a great deal about everything. She stated that he was very rude and ugly to her son. She suspected that Barry did not like male children.)** To add to all the drama, he locked her out of the house by changing the locks, pad locking the refrigerator, and putting all of their furniture in storage to keep her from taking the furniture once he was done with her. The courts made him undo his deceitful acts towards her. Wife number ten walked away with alimony, and there was a binding court order for Barry to pay off her car note as well as retrieve the furniture that he stored away. She stated that she paid for and went on several trips with him as well and that she was almost bankrupt after he tried to "wipe her out", but she pleaded her case to the courts, and was awarded the aforementioned benefits.

- **Wife number nine** called me one day after court because she was out of town. I informed her that I was soliciting affidavits from Barry's former wives and told her that she was a day too late because court was on the day before. <u>We talked and she stated that he was a mentally sick man</u>. <u>This wife stated that he cannot be trusted and that he was so mean and cruel towards her that she never wanted to see him again.</u> **(Awareness: He did the very same things to her that he did to us.) She stated that he did not need another woman he needed a man. <u>She also concurred that he makes sure that all of the wives go to Tennessee, North Carolina, and Canada and that it was like an obsession to him. I was a little shocked because he told me that only his last wife before me went to Canada with him, but I should have known better.</u>**

- <u>He stated that **wife number eleven** was very poor company when they went to Canada together and that it was so much better going there with me.</u> He also stated that he was so glad that we went there together because it made up for the bad times that he had there with her. My sister talked with wife number eleven, and she stated that it took her a while to get over him; therefore, she did not want to open that chapter of her life again. She realized that she had been used, but she just wanted to forget about what happened to her. <u>My understanding is that she signed the paperwork for Barry to purchase a truck, but Barry did not keep it. Instead, he forged her name and later sold it to someone else. This wife also used her money to purchase new cabinets in the kitchen and to wall paper a few rooms in the house.</u> **(Eye opener: My guess is that she did not want to be perceived as being a victim.)** She stated that she had to move on at this point, and I can understand that because he is overwhelmingly crazy.

- I spoke with a church member about **wife number seven** who was in a common law marriage to him, but she birthed a son from Barry. She stated that her friend wanted to stay out of this situation concerning Barry. **(Eye opener: She was another wife who restrained him from the house and received child support for her son when they separated. I spoke with several people about this case and was told that she was once in the military and that he cleaned out her retirement funds after two and one half years.)**

Wife number 6 informed me that he was married to someone by the name of Joslyn before he married her and stated that she married him in South Carolina. I am not one to go by "hearsay", rumor, or gossip, so I recently took a trip to the South Carolina courthouse and discovered that he had married a few wives over there. **(Eye opener: Only a shameless and disgusting man would pretend to be in love with all these women, but his ultimate intent was to con and manipulate us until he had drained us dry; then, after he had exhausted all of our resources, he dumped each one of us for the next victim.)** He reminds me of John 10:10, the thief comes to steal, kill, and destroy. He is a professional thief in every sense of the word.

On February 5, 2010, Dear Journal— My attorney presented all of the facts concerning what Barry had done to me. She pointed out that I had married him twice and that we had a son during our first marriage. Then, we were divorced when he was five months old. She stated that I married him again June 2, 2006, but after a short marriage, he abused my body and depleted my retirement funds. The judge was informed about his multiple marriages; therefore, the judge asked Barry, "How many times have you been married?" He replied, "Ten." During this court session, some significant facts came out about Barry such as his possession of condoms and other sexual objects that were locked in his safe. Another interesting note was that he was secretly conspiring with Denise long distance. The judge recognized that Barry had forced a great deal of debt on me through credit cards along with depleting my retirement funds.

At present, my divorce has not become final because the judge wanted us to attend a mediation to allow us to come to some kind of an agreement without being forced, but Barry refuses to pay off my credit card debt. I have been awarded alimony from the judge from the February 5th court date, but Barry never pays it on time. Nothing that this man does surprises me at this point. <u>I am so very very happy to be out of this relationship. It feels as if I were in a dream, but now I am waking up.</u> **(Awareness: Barry is the kind of person that you meet and everything looks good on the outside, but dark and unexpected things are on the inside. I am the kind of person who has always responded to life spiritually, and sometimes, one can get caught up and involved with someone like Barry who will play you like a fiddle.)** I have learned that the way of the transgressor is hard; Barry's day of reckoning is totally in God's hand. Some people do not know the difference from love and abuse, but when God gets a hold of them, they will repent and reform. I realize that abuse comes in many forms and that it is not only men abusing women, but in a great deal of cases, women abuse men also. I think that one of the most important lessons that I have learned from my marriage to Barry is to pay attention to the RED FLAGS. I will never be as gullible with anyone else as I was with Barry. He came into my life with lots of baggage and did nothing but whine and complain about everyone else when, in fact, "he was the problem all along". Women and men should never put themselves in a position where they are vulnerable and will not take the time to investigate the parties that are interested in them. I admonish anyone who is in a relationship to take the time to investigate marriages and divorces, criminal records, health records, employment records, family ancestry etc. because you never know what you are getting into. If I can leave one thought with you, it will be this one "A MAN'S MIND PLANS HIS WAY." Acknowledge God to direct your path and remember "Marriage Is Good but Get a Background Check."

Resources and References

www.abika.com/Reports/Divorce Records.htm
(Investigate Divorces and Marriages)

www.Datesmart.com/marital.htm
(Lies, Truth, Marriage; investigate your date)

www.1866BackgroundCheck.com
(Find addresses, age, income, criminal history about a person of interest)

www.Acxiom.com/BackgroundCheck
(Criminal Record, Driving Record, Credit Report, Other Verifications)

www.nationalbackgroundcheck.com/
(Employee Background Check)

www.background-checks.sentrylink.com
(Criminal Background Checks and Pre-employment screening)

www.healthcare.com
Investigate health issues

www.BeenVerified.com
(A database of publicly available information)

I did my background checks at the local courthouse and surrounding areas since Barry was a native who never moved away.

About the Author

G eri Lewis is an up-and-coming author who has a degree in Criminal Justice. Many years ago, her deceased mother, Rev. Rosa Lee Cannady, encouraged her to major in this field because she sensed Geri's investigative skills. Later on, her mother strongly suggested that she should write a book not realizing that her first book would be about her life's experiences. When she wrote these journal entries, she wrote them because of her complete concern for her life with Barry the second time around. She was not aware that these journal entries would someday become the basis for this book. Nevertheless, she is very pleased that she took her mother's advice because she was an incredibly wise woman. As you read this book, you will discover that Geri exemplifies a life-giving person, but Barry epitomizes a life-draining person. Despite Geri's many challenges with Barry, she remained spiritual and determined to make her marriage work

CPSIA information can be obtained at www.ICGtesting.com
Printed in the USA
LVOW090531210612

287052LV00002B/258/P